Fun & Easy AMIGURUMI

Contents

Introduction

Amigurumi is of Japanese origin and is the art of creating cute dolls. This book is a collection of crochet patterns from the very best doll designers. Their most beautiful patterns have been brought together in one easy collection.

These patterns assume a basic experience of crochet. With a little crochet knowledge you will find most patterns easy. For each pattern is indicated the level: easy or intermediate. Only one pattern is for experienced crocheters. All patterns are working in continuous rounds.

This book uses US crochet terminology:

Abbreviations

sc = single crochet (UK: double crochet)

Insert the hook into the work (into the second chain from the hook), wrap the yarn over the hook and draw through the work only. Wrap the yarn again and draw the yarn through both loops on the hook.

ch = chain

Wrap the yarn over the hook, pull the yarn through to make a new loop without tightening the first loop.

dc = double crochet (UK: treble crochet)

Wrap yarn over the hook, insert hook into the stitch to be worked. Wrap the yarn over the hook again and pull through the stitch (three loops remain on the hook). Wrap the yarn over the hook and pull through two of the loops on the hook (two loops remain on hook). Wrap the yarn over the hook and pull through the remaining two loops on hook.

hdc = half double crochet (UK: half treble crochet)

Wrap yarn over the hook, insert the hook into the stitch to be worked, wrap the yarn over the hook again and pull through the stitch (three loops remain on the hook). Wrap the yarn over the hook and pull through all three loops on the hook.

sl st = slip stitch

Insert the hook into the work (into second chain from the hook), wrap the yarn over the hook. Draw the yarn through the work and the loop on the hook in one movement.

dec = decrease

Crochet 2 stitches together: insert the hook into the stitch, wrap the yarn over the hook and draw through the work, do the same into the next stitch. Wrap the yarn over the hook and draw through all three loops on the hook.

inc = increase

Make two (or more) stitches into the same stitch.

When crocheting in the round it is a good idea to mark the beginning of a row by placing a short piece of yarn across the work. This will show when you have come to the end of the row. Then pull the piece of yarn out and repositioned it for the next one.

Safety

Even though the plastic eyes used in Amigurumi are often called "safety eyes", they are not approved for use by children under 3. Parts which can come loose like beads, eyes and buttons are unsuitable for children under 3 years old. You can replace these parts with embroidery or crochet. Please ensure that small crocheted parts cannot get loose.

Crochet Owl

"I fell in love with amigurumi about 5 years ago, I love to write simple patterns using basic shapes that can be put together in interesting ways to make something adorable."

by Elizabeth Carr

www.etsy.com/uk/shop/Lybo

Skill level:

EASY

2 FINE

Materials:

1. Oddments of yarn in four different colours. I used sport weight cotton (UK 4-ply).
2. Two 6 mm plastic safety eyes.
3. Small amount of polyester stuffing.
4. Blunt-ended darning needle.
5. Crochet hook, size C-2 (UK 2.5 mm).
6. Fabric glue.

You can use thicker yarn if you like, your owl will just come out slightly bigger. Remember to increase the size of your crochet hook, you may also need slightly larger eyes.

Abbreviations:

sc   = single crochet
hdc   = half double crochet
dc   = double crochet
ch   = chain
dec 1 = decrease 1 (join 2 sts into 1)
sl st   = slip stitch
* * around = repeat the steps between the asterisks
( )   = total number of stitches in a round/row
R   = Round
( )   = different type of sts in 1 st

Eyes
Make 2
R1: ch 2, 6 sc into second ch from hook.
R2: 2 sc into each sc around. (12 stitches)
Fasten off and sew in the ends.

Eyes

Body

R1: ch 2, 6 sc into second ch from hook.
R2: 2 sc into each sc around. (12)
R3: *sc 1, 2 sc in next sc*, repeat 6 times. (18)
R4: *sc 2, 2 sc in next sc*, repeat 6 times. (24)
R5: *sc 3, 2 sc in next sc*, repeat 6 times. (30)
R6-8: sc 30.
R9: *sc 3, dec 1*, repeat 6 times. (24)
R10-12: sc 24.
R13: *sc 2, dec 1*, repeat 6 times. (18)
R14: sc 18.
R15: sc 3, hdc, dc, hdc, sc 6, hdc, dc, hdc, sc 3. *Fasten off.*

6

Beak

R1: ch 2, sc into second chain from hook, ch 1 (turning chain).

R2: sc 2, sl st into first sc in row to shape beak.

Fasten off.

Wings

Make 2

R1: ch 6

R2: sl st into second ch from hook, then working down the chain: sc, hdc, dc, (hdc, sl st, hdc) into last ch.

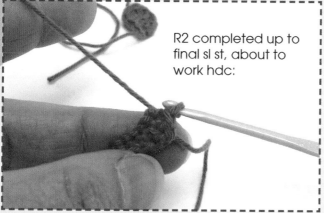

R2 completed up to final sl st, about to work hdc:

R3: working down the other side of the original ch: dc, hdc, sc, sl st. *Fasten off.*

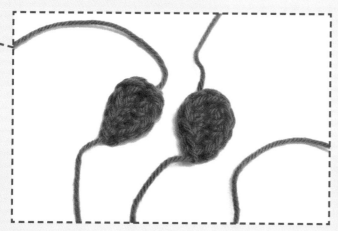

Feet

Make 2

R1: ch 4, sl st into first ch to make a ring.

R2: *ch 4, then starting with second ch from hook, sl st 3. Sl st into next ch of original ring* repeat 3 more times.

Fasten off.

You will have a cross shape, gently reshape so there are 3 "toes" at the front and one at the back. Make a couple of stitches to hold front 3 toes together.

Assembling the Parts

Do this carefully, pining each piece in position before you sew it to make absolutely sure that you are happy with your owls expression!

1. Push the plastic eyes through the centre of the crochet eye circle, then push through the body. Make sure you are happy with the position before attaching the safety back. If you like you can dab a little fabric glue around the underside of the crochet eye circle to stop it from curling up - this isn't always necessary - wait until you have stuffed the body and see if you need to.

2. Stuff your owl with the polyester filling. Then over-sew along the top of his head, gently shaping his ears.

3. Attach the beak between the eyes, sew in place, and if necessary add a dab of fabric glue to keep it in place.

4. Sew the feet in position, you will probably need a little fabric glue to make sure they stay in the correct position, pin them in place while the glue dries.

5. Finally, sew the wings in place, again add a dab of fabric glue to secure them if needed.

Lana Dolls

by Vanja Grundmann
AmigurumiBB
www.amigurumibb.com

Skill level:

EASY

Materials:

1. Sport weight (5 ply) cotton yarn in:
   - Skin color of your choice.
   - Favorite color for dress, shoes and headband.
   - White colored yarn (or ecru) for panties.
   - Mixed colors for flowers, tiny bits of greens for leaves.
   - Colour of your choice for hair.
2. Super Fine or Fingering (No 1) cotton yarn in white for edgings and flower on dress.
3. Embroidery thread or lace weight yarn (No 0) in red color for the mouth.
4. 2 mm crochet hook.
5. Darning or tapestry needle for sewing.
6. Textile glue.
7. Pins.
8. Marker.
9. Stuffing of your choice.
10. White pencil if you decide to add make up on doll's eyes.
11. Fine point ball pen or marker in black color also for doll's eyes.

2 FINE

Size:

Lana is 18 cm tall. (7")

Abbreviations:

sc = single crochet
hdc = half double crochet
dc = double crochet
ch = chain
inc = increasing stitch (2 stitches made in one stitch)
dec = decreasing stitch (2 stitches worked together)
sl st = slip stitch
* * = repeat steps between the asterisks
x2 = 2 times
( ) = total number of stitches in a round and sometimes used for the number of rounds.
st(s) = stitche(s)
R = rounds

Other stitches used in the pattern:

- 4dc cluster stitch (thumb on doll's hand)
- running stitch (shoes): This is a surface crochet technique to decorate. Create a round of slip stitches working around the post of each stitch of the last round.

Head

R1: sc6 in magic ring (6)
R2: inc x6 (12)
R3: *inc, sc* x6 (18)
R4: *inc, sc2* x6 (24)
R5: *inc, sc3* x6 (30)
R6: *inc, sc4* x6 (36)
R7: *inc, sc5* x6 (42)
R8: *inc, sc6* x6 (48)
R9-R16: sc48
R17: *inc, sc* x10, sc28 (58)
R18: sc30, dec, sc5, *dec, sc4* x2, dec, sc5, dec (53)
R19: sc53
R20: sc30, dec, sc4, *dec, sc2* x2, dec, sc5, dec (48)
R21: sc48
R22: *dec, sc* x10, sc18 (38)
R23: sc38
R24: dec x10, sc18 (28)
R25: *dec, sc* x4, dec, *dec, sc* x4, dec (18)
R26: *dec, sc* x6 (12)

Fasten off, leaving long tail for sewing (embroidering nose later). Stuff head nice and very firm.
Keep in mind that you are making a doll, not a plush. Crocheted dolls tend to be stuffed well. Take your time stuffing the head. Only well stuffed it will keep the nice round shape.

Sewing Nose

Use the tail (yarn) left from making the head. Thread the needle. Mark the very center stitch on R16 of the head. Going from bottom head opening, bring the needle to marked stitch and wave the yarn over this stitch for 2-3 times. Finish by taking the needle out from the bottom head opening, cut and hide yarn inside the head's stuffing. Your tiny little nose is done.

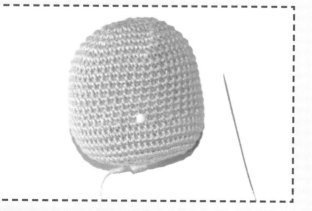

Feet and legs

Start with ch6.
R1: starting from the second chain stitch work in one chain loop; sc4, 3sc in the last chain stitch, continue working around chain, sc3, 2sc in one st (12)
R2: inc, sc3, *hdc inc* x3, sc3, inc2 (18)
R3: back loops only: sc 18
R4: sc18
R5: sc6, dec3, sc6 (15)
R6: dec, sc4, dec, sc5, dec (12)
R7: sc3, dec3, sc3 (9)
Stuff the feet nice and firm.
R8-R19: sc9 (12 rounds)
Fasten off, stuff legs.

Connecting legs and working the body

Work with white or ecru color yarn. As we connect the legs we will be making the doll's panties. Bring both legs together, toes pointing same direction. Starting with left leg, attach white yarn to the stitch right after your last working stitch of the leg. Start crocheting next leg, making 9sc. One leg is finished.

Your next stitch will be made on the opposite leg. Single crochet first free stitch from the stitch where you attached white yarn (look at the 1st photo on the next page). Continue making 7 more single crochet stitches on this leg. Finish the round making last stitch at the same stitch where white yarn was attached.

R1: sc9 (first leg) + sc9 (second leg) (18)

R2: *inc, sc2* x6 (24)
R3: sc24
R4: *inc, sc3* x6 (30)
R5-R6: sc30

On last stitch of R6, change yarn to skin color.

R7: back loops only: sc30
R8-R9: sc30
R10: *dec, sc3* x6 (24)
R11-R13: sc24
R14: *dec, sc2* x6 (18)
R15-R17: sc18
R18: *dec, sc* x6 (12)
R19-R20: sc12

Fasten off leaving long tail for sewing body and head together later.

Before you stuff the body, return to panties and with white yarn add a little lace looking edge:

Edge of Panties

Working on front loops of R7, attach white yarn to any of front loops and work the following pattern to create tiny little edging on doll's panties

ch2, skip one stitch, slip stitch to next stitch repeat around.

Finish off, hide ends.

You can stuff doll's body now. Stuff nice and firm. After stuffing, sew body and head together. Set head pointing right direction and sew nicely around 12 stitches on each of two pieces.
Before closing the round completely, add some more stuffing to make neck nice and firm.

Shoe

In color of your choice.
Start with ch6.
R1: starting from the second chain stitch work in one chain loop; sc4, 3sc in the last chain stitch, continue working around chain, sc3, 2sc in one st (12)
R2: inc, sc3, *hdc inc* x3, sc3, inc2 (18)
R3: sc, inc, sc4, *hdc inc, hdc* x2, hdc inc, sc4, inc, sc, inc (24)
R4: back loops only: sc24
R5-R6: sc24

R7: dec, sc6, dec4, sc6, dec (18)
Fasten off and hide ends.
Using white color yarn make running stitch across the last round of stitches.

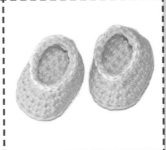

Arms

Make 2
R1: sc6 in magic ring (6)
R2: inc x6 (12)
R3-R4: sc12
R5: 4 dc cluster stitch, sc11 (12)
R6: *dec, sc* x4 (8)
Stuff the fist before continuing with upper arm.
R7-R21: sc8

Fasten off leaving long tail for sewing arm to the body. Stuff arm. Sew arms on sides of the body, on 3rd round from top.

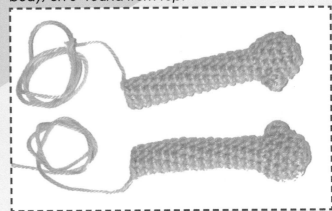

Dress

Using color of your choice.
Starting with chain ch18, mark last stitch, make 7 more chains (these will be used for button loop). Work R1-11 in rows. Ch1 and turn after each row is finished.

R1: starting from the marked stitch (18th on your chain) sc18 (18)
R2: *inc, sc* x9 (27)
R3: *inc, sc2* x9 (36)
R4: *inc, sc3* x9 (45)
R5: *inc, sc4* x9 (54)
R6: sc8, ch6, skip 11 sts over R5 and sc to 12th st, sc 15 more stitches, ch6, skip 11 sts over R5 and sc to 12th st, sc 7 more stitches (32sts + 12 chain sts)
R7: sc8, sl st first chain st, dec x2, sl st last chain st, sc16, sl st first chain st, dec x2, sl st last chain st, sc8 (36 sts + 4 sl sts)
R8: sc8, skip sl st, sc2, skip sl st, sc16, skip sl st, sc2, skip sl st, sc8 (36)
R9: sc12, *inc, sc* x6, sc12 (42)
R10: sc15, *inc, sc* x6, sc15 (48)
R11: sc48, sl st to first stitch in order to create circle.

From next round we will work in rounds, but each round will start with ch1 and finish with slip stitch to this chain. This way our edge will remain straight.

R12-R21: sc48 (10 rounds)
R22: Work in front loops only. *ch2, skip one stitch, sl st to next* repeat around. This round creates nice lacy edge on the dress's bottom.

Fasten off.

In the back loops of R22, attach fingering yarn in white color.
Skip 1 st, 4sc in the next st, skip one st, sl st to next st repeat around.

Fasten off and hide ends.

Collar

Attach white, fingering yarn to first stitch of chain made when starting the dress.

R1: *inc, sc2* x6 (24)
R2: sc10, hdc x4 in next st, sl st to next two stitches, hdc x4 in the following stitch, sc10.

Fasten off and hide end.

Hide all visible yarns. Sew tiny little button on the back of the dress, making sure it matches same row as your loop.

Front view

Back view

Flower

This flower is for the dress and headband.
Working in magic loop:
R1: sc1, *ch3, sc1* x4, ch3, sl st to first sc made.

Fasten off leaving tail long enough for sewing it on the dress or headband.

Close the magic ring.

Sew the flower on chest part of the dress.

Leaf

This leaf is for the headband.
Start with ch6.
R1: sl st to the second chain stitch from hook, sc x2, hdc, hdc x3 in the last chain stitch, continue working around chain, hdc, sc x2, sl st.

Fasten off, leaving long tail for sewing.

Arrange ends so they stay on the back side of the leaf.

Sew the leaf on the headband later.

Eyes

Using black yarn.
R1: sc7 in magic ring

Fasten off. Hide ends in the back and cut them short.

Thread the needle with white thread or white fingering yarn. On top left corner of each eye embroider tiny little dot. Simply wave the yarn around corner of one stitch for two times and your white dot or spark is done.

Attaching the white color yarn to make border on dress's end.

Attaching yarn to make the collar.

Place your eyes right above nose line, leaving 8 stitches between them.

Make sure the sparks (white dots) are pointing the same direction when placing eyes on the face.

Apply glue on the back of each eye and place it safe with safety pins. Leave for at least one hour to dry.

While waiting for glue to dry, you have time to embroider mouth. Use lace weight yarn or thread to create mouth. No matter how thin the yarn is, it will always be visible on the doll's head. Use photo below as your guide for embroidering the mouth. Mouth is placed two rounds below nose. The corners of the mouth are parallel with inner eye edges. Bottom line of the mouth is hardly going two rounds below.

Another option to make lips is a tiny little vertical line (over one stitch), on fourth round below and parallel with nose. An example of such a mouth you can see on the pink dressed doll.

Eye make up (optional)

Once the eyes are dried and your pins are removed, you can use a white color pencil. Apply white pencil right above the eye. It will make face and eye look as having make up and will brighten the little black dots we crocheted as eyes.

Then use a fine point marker or black ball point and starting from top of each eye, draw a tiny little line on each of the inner side of eye. Draw the very fine line, hardly visible, but yet it makes a difference: it brings depth and shape to simple black yarn eyes.

Hair

With color of your choice.

R1: sc4 in magic ring (4)

Do not close the ring. Hair is worked in rows. After each row ch1 and turn.

R2: inc4 (8)
R3: *inc, sc* x4 (12)
R4: *inc, sc2* x4 (16)

R5: *inc, sc3* x4 (20)
R6: *inc, sc4* x4 (24)
R7: *inc, sc5* x4 (28)
R8: *inc, sc6* x4 (32)
R9-R16: sc32

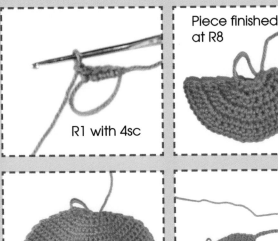

R1 with 4sc

Piece finished at R8

R16 finished

R17: ch26, starting on the first hair lock

R17: in addition to ch1 and turn, ch25 more stitches

Hair locks

lock 1: Starting from the second chain stitch from hook make 2 sc in each of next 10 chain stitches, continue with 2 hdc in each of next 10 chain stitches, finish with 2dc in each of the next 5 sts. Your first lock is done. Secure it to the base of R16 in the following way: Skip 3 stitches, slip stitch to 4th stitch.

lock 2: Start with ch26 and then do the same as for Lock 1

lock 3: Same as Lock 2

So far you have three locks of the same size done. The next two locks are 5 stitches longer.

Longer back lock1: ch31, starting from the second chain stitch, work 2sc in each of the next 10 stitches, continue with 2hdc in each of the next 10 stitches, finish with 2dc in next 10 chain stitches. Skip 3 sts on the R16 and slip stitch to next (4th stitch).

Longer back lock 2: same as Longer back lock1

Now that you finished the long locks on the back, you continue with same size locks you made at the start of this row.

Locks 4, 5 & 6: same as short lock 2.

On the last lock, after making last slip stitch on R16, finish off and hide end.

inc sc worked over chain

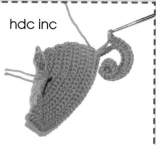

hdc inc

lock finishes with dc inc and slip stitch to R16

Back of the hair piece finished

Front side of hair piece (fringes)

Attach yarn to magic loop

R1: sc3 (3)

Work in rows, after finishing each row, make ch1 and turn and start with next row.

R2: inc3 (6)

R3: *inc, sc* x3 (9)

R4: *inc, sc2* x3 (12)

R5: *inc, sc3* x3 (15)

R6: *inc, sc4* x3 (18)

R7: *inc, sc5* x3 (21)

R8: *inc, sc6* x3 (24)

R9-R11: sc24

R12: dec, sc4, dec, sc2, dec x2, sc2, dec, sc4, dec (18) *Fasten off and hide end.*

Close the magic ring, secure and tie ends inside the head wig.

Your hair is done. You can place it on doll's head. To attach hair on the head you will need textile glue. Here are few steps on how the glue is applied and the hair placed on the head.

Apply glue on the inside of the entire back hair piece, front, top and edges. Do not apply glue on locks.

Center the hair piece on the head by placing a pin through magic ring of the hair and head.

Stretch the hair over the head and pin it.

At the end, arrange the fringes. Edges must match the edge on each hair side. Pin them on the sides and let the glue dry.

Headband

Working in color of your choice. Leave long tail at the beginning.

Start by making 37 chain stitches.

R1: starting at the second chain stitch from the hook, sl st 6, sc6, hdc 12, sc 6, sl st 6

Fasten off leaving long tail for sewing. Sew headband on sides of dolls head (over hair).

You can attach flower and leaf before adding headband on the head, or you can add them later. Instead of one flower, you can add several.

Your Lana Doll is now complete!

Vinnie, the Teddy Bear

"Vinnie is playful, adventurous, funny and loving. If you go outside with this little bear be careful, you never know what adventures he will take you on. But at night, you will have sweet dreams hugging him."

by Gemma Cubells
www.tremenducrochet.com

Skill level:

INTERMEDIATE

Materials:

1. Worsted weight yarn in broken white and brown color
2. Size G (4 mm) crochet hook
3. Black embroidery floss
4. Small piece of black craft felt and matching sewing thread
5. Sharp embroidery needle
6. Tapestry needle
7. Fiberfill or stuffing of your choice
8. Stitch marker
9. 13 mm plastic eyes with safety backings

4 MEDIUM

Size:

Vinnie the Teddy Bear is 11" tall. (28 cm)

Abbreviations:

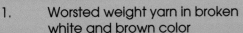

sc   = single crochet
ch   = chain
dec   = single crochet decrease
* * repeat = repeat steps between asterisks
( )   = total number of stitches in a round
st(s)   = stitche(s)
R   = round(s)

Arms

Make 2. Using G hook and brown yarn.

R1: ch 2, 6 sc in second ch from hook.
R2: sc 2 in each sc around. (12)
R3: *sc 5, 2 sc in next sc*, repeat 2 times. (14)
R4-R5: sc 14.
R6: *sc 5, dec 1*, repeat 2 times. (12)
R7: *sc 1, dec 1*, repeat 4 times. (8)
R8-R10: sc 8.

Slightly stuff hand and continue crocheting.

R11-R17: sc 8.

Fasten off, leaving long tail for sewing and set aside.

Legs

Make 2. Starting at bottom of foot, using G hook and brown yarn.

R1: ch 6, sc 5 starting in second chain from hook, then work 5 sc on opposite side of chain. (10)
R2: 2 sc in first stitch, sc 3, 2 sc in next 2 sts, sc 3, 2 sc in last stitch. (14)
R3: sc 1, 2 sc in next st, sc 4, 2 sc in next st, sc 1, 2 sc in next st, sc 4, 2 sc in last st. (18)
R4-R5: sc 18.
R6: sc 2, dec 2, sc 6, dec 2, sc 2. (14)
R7: sc 5, dec 2, sc 5. (12)
R8: sc 12.

Stuff foot and continue crocheting.

R9-R17: sc 12.

Stuff leg and continue crocheting.

R18 for right leg: sc 6. Fasten off, leaving long tail for sewing and set aside.

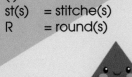

R18 for left leg: ch 3, sc in each st of the last right leg round (12 sts), sc 3 (working on ch sts), sc 12 (left leg stitches), sc 3 (working on ch sts). (30)

Move the st marker to indicate the new beginning of round.

Do not fasten off, proceed to next round to begin the body.

How to: join legs with a short separation

1. Let's look at how to join the legs in detail:

2. Make ch 3 on the leg your yarn is attached to (the left leg of your plushie).

3. Sc in each st of the last right leg round, starting into the next st you fasten off the yarn.

4. Sc 3 working on chain stitches, continue sc in each stitch of the last left leg round.

5. Sc 3 working on the opposite side of the chain.

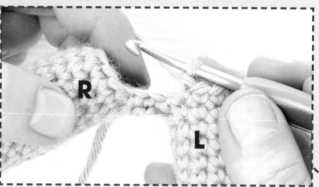

5. You did it! The legs are now joined. Continue crocheting the next round.

Body

R19: *sc 4, 2 sc in next sc*, repeat 6 times. (36)
R20: *sc 5, 2 sc in next sc*, repeat 6 times. (42)
R21: *sc 6, 2 sc in next sc*, repeat 6 times. (48)
R22: *sc 7, 2 sc in next sc*, repeat 6 times. (54)
R23-R25: sc 54.
R26: *sc 7, dec 1*, repeat 6 times. (48)
R27-R28: sc 48.
R29: *sc 6, dec 1*, repeat 6 times. (42)
R30-R32: sc 42.
R33: *sc 5, dec 1*, repeat 6 times. (36)
R34-R36: sc 36.
R37: *sc 4, dec 1*, repeat 6 times. (30)
R38-R40: sc 30.

Stuff body and continue crocheting.

R41: *sc 3, dec 1*, repeat 6 times. (24)
R42: sc 24.
R43: *sc 2, dec 1*, repeat 6 times. (18)

R44: sc 18.

Fasten off and weave in ends.
Flatten arms and attach to body at round 41.
Add a little more stuffing and set aside.

Belly

Using G hook and broken white yarn.
R1: ch 2, 2 sc in second ch from hook.
R2: ch 1, turn, sc 1, 2 sc in next sc. (3)
R3: ch 1, turn, *2 sc in next sc*, repeat 3 times. (6)
R4: ch 1, turn, sc 6. (6)
R5: ch 1, turn, *Sc 1, 2 sc in next sc*, repeat 3 times. (9)
R6: ch 1, turn, sc 4, 2 sc in next sc, sc 4. (10)
R7: ch 1, turn, sc 10. (10)
R8: ch 1, turn, sc 3, 2 sc in next sc, sc 2, 2 sc in next sc, sc 3. (12)
R9: ch 1, turn, sc 12. (12)
R10: ch 1, turn, sc 1, dec 1, *sc 2, dec 1* repeat 2 times, sc 1. (9)
R11: ch 1, turn, sc 1, dec 1, sc 3, dec 1, sc 1. (7)
R12: ch 1, turn, *sc 1, dec 1* repeat 2 times, sc 1. (5)
R13: ch 1, turn, dec 1, sc 1, dec 1. (3)

Fasten off, leaving long tail for sewing and sew to body.

Tail

Using G hook and brown yarn.
R1: ch 2, 6 sc in second ch from hook.
R2: sc 2 in each sc around. (12)
R3: sc 12.
R4: *dec 1*, repeat 6 times. (6)

Fasten off, leaving long tail for sewing.
Slightly stuff tail and sew to body.

Head

Using G hook and brown yarn.
R1: ch 2, 6 sc in second ch from hook.
R2: sc 2 in each sc around. (12)
R3: *sc 1, 2 sc in next sc*, repeat 6 times. (18)
R4: *sc 2, 2 sc in next sc*, repeat 6 times. (24)
R5: *sc 3, 2 sc in next sc*, repeat 6 times. (30)
R6: *sc 4, 2 sc in next sc*, repeat 6 times. (36)
R7: *sc 5, 2 sc in next sc*, repeat 6 times. (42)
R8: *sc 6, 2 sc in next sc*, repeat 6 times. (48)
R9: *sc 7, 2 sc in next sc*, repeat 6 times. (54)
R10: *sc 8, 2 sc in next sc*, repeat 6 times. (60)
R11-R19: sc 60.
R20: *sc 8, dec 1*, repeat 6 times. (54)
R21: *sc 7, dec 1*, repeat 6 times. (48)
R22: *sc 6, dec 1*, repeat 6 times. (42)
R23: *sc 5, dec 1*, repeat 6 times. (36)
R24: *sc 4, dec 1*, repeat 6 times. (30)
R25: *sc 3, dec 1*, repeat 6 times. (24)

Work on face: position and attach eyes.
Stuff head and continue crocheting.

R26: *sc 2, dec 1*, repeat 6 times. (18)

Fasten off, leaving long tail for sewing and sew to body.

Muzzle

Using G hook and broken white yarn.
R1: ch 2, 6 sc in second ch from hook.
R2: sc 2 in each sc around. (12)
R3: sc 12.
R4: *sc 1, 2 sc in next sc*, repeat 6 times. (18)
R5-R10: sc 18.
R11: *sc 1, dec 1*, repeat 6 times. (12)
R12: sc 12.

Slightly stuff muzzle and continue crocheting.

R13: *dec 1*, repeat 6 times. (6)
R14: sc next and 4th st together.

Fasten off, leaving long tail for sewing and sew

to head.

Work on face: *for the nose cut a piece of black felt (triangular piece with rounded ends) and sew to muzzle. With black embroidery floss make a line under the nose.*

Ears

Make 2.

Let's get started making the inside piece of the ear, using G hook and broken white yarn.

R1: ch 2, 6 sc in second ch from hook.

R2: sc 2 in each sc around. (12)

Fasten off, weave in ends and set aside.

Now let's make the outside part of the ear, using G hook and brown yarn.

R1: ch 2, 6 sc in second ch from hook.

R2: sc 2 in each sc around. (12)

Now, take the broken white piece of the ear (the one you have just made) and put wrong sides of each piece together.

Continue crocheting round 3, working one stitch of each piece at the same time.

R3: sc 12 (working the two pieces at the same time).

R4: sc 12.

Fasten off, leaving long tail for sewing and sew to head.

Congratulations: you did it!

I hope you enjoy

your new plushie.

by Teerapon Chan-lam (Jenny)
www.jennyandteddy.com

Abbreviations:

You will need to know how to make a magic ring or adjustable ring.

mr	=	magic ring
sc	=	single crochet
st	=	stitch
ch	=	chain
inc 1	=	increase 1 (2 sc in next st)
dec 1	=	decrease 1 (join 2 sts into 1)
sl st	=	slip stitch
* * around	=	repeat steps
( )	=	total no. of sts in a round/row
R	=	round

Skill level:

EASY

Size:

The animals are about 3-3.5 inch (7.5 – 9 cm) tall in sitting position. The size varies depending on the size of yarn and crochet hook.

Materials:

2 FINE

1. Acrylic yarn, you can use 8 ply yarn.
2. Plastic eyes with safety backing: 7.5 mm
3. Fiberfill for stuffing
4. Sewing needle
5. Ribbon
6. Crochet hook size: 1.25 mm
7. Craft glue

The size of the crochet hook really does not matter. The doll design will work out just fine with different sizes of crochet hooks. Only the end size of the creation will differ slightly.

In this pattern, you will be working in the round continuously. You may use a short piece of contrasting colour yarn to mark the beginning of each round.

When you end a round, do not join at the end of each round; you will begin the second round in the next stitch.

At the end of each round, I have given the number of stitches you should have. If you are off by 1 or 2 stitches, do not worry about it.

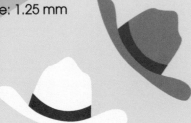

Head

For the Tiger use yellow yarn, Cat use light yellow and do the Pig in pink.
Working from top to bottom.
R1: MR (magic ring) and 6sc in ring (6)
R2: 2sc in each st around (12)
R3: *sc in next st, 2sc in next st* repeat around (18)
R4: *sc in next 2 st, 2sc in next st* repeat around(24)
R5: *sc in next 3 st, 2sc in next st* repeat around (30)
R6: *sc in next 4 st, 2sc in next st* repeat around (36)
R7-13: sc in each st around (36)
R14: *sc in each of next 4 st, dec 1* repeat around (30)
R15: *sc in each of next 3 st, dec 1* repeat around (24)
R16: *sc in each of next 2 st, dec 1* repeat around (18)
R17: *sc in each of next st, dec 1* repeat around (12)

Finish off and leave long end for sewing.
Stuff firmly with polyester.

Take a break to make a face for the monkey first.

R14: *sc in each of next 4 st, dec 1* repeat around (30)
R15: *sc in each of next 3 st, dec 1* repeat around (24)
R16: *sc in each of next 2 st, dec 1* repeat around (18)
Start to stuff with polyester stuffing.

R17: *sc in next st, dec 1* repeat around until the hole is closed. Counting st is not important in this round.
Finish off. Leave long tail for sewing.

Head for monkey

Work from top to bottom.
With skin colour.
R1: MR and 6sc in ring (6)
R2: 2sc in each st around (12)
R3: *sc in next st, 2sc in next st* repeat around (18)
R4: *sc in next 2 st, 2sc in next st* repeat around (24)
R5: *sc in next 3 st, 2sc in next st* repeat around (30)
R6: *sc in next 4 st, 2sc in next st* repeat around (36)
R7: sc in each st around (36)

Change to orange yarn.
R8-13: sc in each st around (36)

Arms and legs

Make 4 identical pieces for each animal.
With yellow for Tiger, orange for Monkey and pink for the Pig.
R1: MR and 8sc in ring (8)
R2-12: sc in each st around (8)

Finish off and leave long end for sewing.
Stuff just a little with polyester fiberfill.

Arms and Legs for Cat

Make 4 pieces

With brown:
R1: MR and 8sc in ring (8)
R2-3: sc in each st around (8)
Change to light yellow
R4-12: sc in each st around (8)
Finish off and leave long end for sewing. Stuff a little with fiberfill.

Ears for Tiger and Monkey

Make 2 in yellow for Tiger and orange for Monkey.

R1: MR and 5sc in ring (5)
R2: 2sc in each st around (10)
R3: *Sc in next st, 2sc in next st* repeat around (15)
R4-6: sc in each st around (15)
Finish off. Leave long end for sewing. Do not stuff.

For tiger ears: sew top and end of the ear closed.

Ears for Cat and Piggy

Make 2 in pink for Piggy and brown for Cat.

R1: MR and 3sc in ring (3)
R2: 2sc in each st around (6)
R3: *Sc in next st, 2sc in next st* repeat around (9)
R4: *Sc in next 2 st, 2sc in next st* repeat around (12)
R5-7: sc in each st around (12)
Finish off. Leave long end for sewing. Do not stuff.

Nose for Pig, Monkey and Cat

Make 2. White for Piggy & Monkey. Brown for Cat.

R1: MR and 5sc in ring (5)
R2: 2sc in each st around (10)
R3: sc in each st around (10)
Finish off and leave long tail for sewing.

Nose for Tiger

With white colour
Start with chain 7 (7)
R1-2: sc in each st around (12)

Finish off and leave long tail for sewing .
Do not stuff.

Body

With yellow for Tiger, brown for Cat, orange for
Monkey, pink for Pig. You will work from bottom to top.

R1: MR and 6sc in ring (6)
R2: 2sc in each st around (12)
R3: *sc in next st, 2sc in next st* repeat around (18)
R4: *sc in next 2 st, 2sc in next st* repeat around (24)
R5-8: sc in each st around (24)
R9: *sc in each of next 4 st, dec 1* repeat around (20)
R10-11: sc in each st around (20)
R12: *sc in each of next 3 st, dec 1* repeat around (16)
R13: *sc in each of next 2 st, dec 1* repeat around (12)
Finish off and leave long end for sewing.
Stuff firmly with polyester.

Tail

With yellow for Tiger, brown for Cat,
orange for Monkey
Start with 11 chains (11)
R1: sc in next 10 st from hook. (10)
Finish off and leave long tail for sewing.

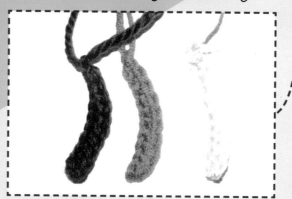

Tail for Piggy

In pink

Start with 9 chains and finish off leaving
long tail for sewing. (9)

Finishing

Sew nose to the face and ears to the head.
Then attach body to the head, arms and legs.

For scarf use fabric in colour of your choice
and cut it in a V shape.

Bear Bunnies

For our little ones with love.

"I have been into arts and crafts since my first memories. All my life I have been creating something: drawing, painting, DIY, sculpture, pottery, anything you can imagine. With Amigurumi I started at the beginning of 2013. I discovered it by accident: I was working on a chameleon doll for one of my nieces. That is how it all started. With one tiny chameleon!

I just love making Amigurumi. To me it feels as putting together painting (the color), sculpture (creating the shape), crafting (crocheting itself). So it fills me completely and makes me very, very happy. Final satisfaction is seeing a wide smile on children's faces having in their hands one of my creations. That is priceless!"

by Vanja Grundmann
www.amigurumibb.com

Skill level:

EASY

Materials:

1. Sport weight cotton yarn in: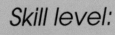
   - white
   - color of your choice
   - tiny bits of contrasting yarn for the flower
   - string of brown yarn for nose and mouth embroidery
2. 2 mm crochet hook
3. 5 mm safety eyes or black round beads to use for eyes
4. needle for sewing parts together
5. stuffing of your choice
6. powder blush for the cheeks

This project is working in continuous rounds, do not join or turn unless otherwise stated. Mark first stitch of each round.

Abbreviations:

ch	=	chain
sc	=	single crochet
st	=	stitch
sl st	=	slip stitch
inc	=	increasing stitch (2 stitches made in one stitch)
dec	=	decreasing stitch (two stitches together)
hdc	=	half double crochet
dc	=	double crochet
R	=	Round
x2	=	2 times
( )	=	total no. of sts in a round
* *	=	repeat stitches between the asterisks

For the tail you can use a popcorn stitch.

Head

In white, start with: ch9

R1: sc x7, 3 sc in one st, continue working around chain, sc x6, 2 sc in one st (18)
R2: inc, sc x6, inc x3, sc x6, inc x2 (24)
R3: inc, sc x9, inc x3, sc x9, inc x2 (30)
R4: inc, sc x12, inc x3, sc x12, inc x2 (36)
R5: inc, sc x15, inc x3, sc x15, inc x2 (42)
R6: inc, sc x18, inc x3, sc x18, inc x2 (48)
R7: inc, sc x21, inc x3, sc x21, inc x2 (54)
R8-R17: sc x54 sts

If using safety eyes, place them in between rounds 11-12, leaving 5 stitches between them.

R18: dec, sc x21, dec x3, sc x21, dec x2 (48)
R19: sc x48 sts
R20: *dec, sc x4* x8 (40)
R21: *sc x2, dec* x10 (30)
R22: *dec, sc* x10 (20)
R23: *sc x8, dec* x2 (18) - On the last stitch change the color to the one you'll use for the body.

The head is finished: stuff it nice and firm

Body

Use a colour of your choice

R1: inc x3, sc x6, inc x3, sc x6 (24)
R2-R3: sc x24 sts
R4: sc, inc x3, sc x9, inc x3, sc x8 (30)
R5-R6: sc x30 sts
R7: sc x2, inc x3, sc x12, inc x3, sc x10 (36)
R8-R9: sc x36 sts
R10: sc x4, inc x3, sc x15, inc x3, sc x11 (42)
R11-R17: sc x42 sts
R18: sc x40 sts

Your last stitch should meet the center of the body piece.

This is the time to test your work:
Fold body to find center. If the stitch doesn't meet the center, you may need to add or remove a stitch or two.

Mark first st of Round 19 as this will be your beginning of each round on the leg.

R19: sc x19, dec (20)

Stuff the body and continue stuffing as you work on your leg.

R20: sc x8, dec x2, sc x8 (18)
R21: sc x18
R22: sc x7, dec x2, sc x7 (16)
R23: sc x16
R24: sc x7, dec x2, sc x5 (14)
R25: sc x14
R26: sc x6, dec x2, sc x4 (12)
R27: sc x12

Begin stuffing the leg and continue for the next two rounds.

R28: sc x5, dec x2, sc x2 (10)
R29: sc x10
R30: sc x2, dec x4, sc x1 (6)

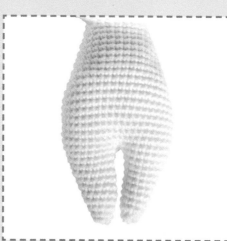

Fasten off, sew last round closed.

Second leg: Starting from the stitch in the center of the body, proceed following R19-R30.

Arms

Make 2 in white

R1: sc x6 in magic ring
R2: *inc, sc x2* x2 (8)
R3: sc x8 sts
R4: dec, sc x2, inc x2, sc x2 (9)
R5: dec, sc x3, inc, sc x3 (9)
R6: sc x4, inc, sc x4 (10)
R7-R9: sc x10 sts
R10: sc x5, inc, sc x4 (11)
R11-R12: sc x11 sts
R13: sc x6, inc, sc x4 (12)
R14-R15: sc x12 sts

Stuff arm.

R16: *dec, sc* x4 (8)

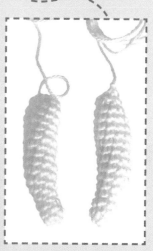

Fasten off leaving long end for sewing arms to body. Sew arms on side of the body on the second round of the body.

Ears

Make 2
Ears are done in two pieces: Inner and outer part. Outer part is done in white and inner part in the colour of the body. You can mix colours or use completely different colours.

Outer Part

Make 2
Start with: ch16
R1: sc x11, hdc x3, 3hdc in last chain stitch, work around chain, hdc x3, sc x11 (31)
ch1, turn
R2: sc x8, hdc x6, inc hdc x3, hdc x6, sc x8 (34)
ch1, turn
R3: sc x34 sts

Fasten off leaving long end for sewing.
R1 & R3 are facing right side of your work.

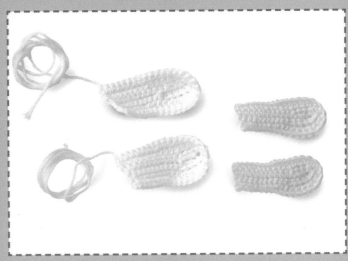

Inner Part

(Make 2)
Start with: ch16
R1: sc x11, hdc x3, 3hdc in last chain stitch, work around chain, hdc x3, sc x11 (31)
ch1, turn
R2: sc x8, hdc x6, inc hdc x3, hdc x6, sc x8 (34)
Fasten off and hide the ends.
R2 is facing your right side for this ear piece.

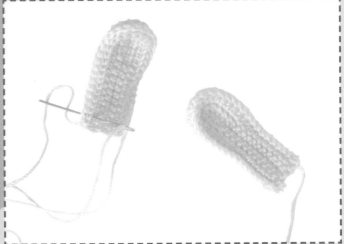

Bring inner and outer ear part together, wrong sides facing each other. With tail left on outer ear part using wipe stitch, sew around through all of 34 stitches.

Sew ears on top of the head, starting on the edge stitches of the first round.

Nose

In white
R1: sc x5 in magic ring
R2: inc x5 (10 sts)
R3: *inc, sc* x5 (15 sts)
R4: *inc, sc x2* x5 (20 sts)
R5: sc20

Fasten off leaving long tail.

Position top of the nose on the same round where eyes are placed. Stuff it lightly, pin and sew nicely on the head.

After sewing, thread the needle with brown color yarn and embroider nose and mouth. Use photo as your guide.

Tail

Start with: ch4
Make popcorn stitch with 5 dc in the forth chain from hook, fasten off leaving long tail for sewing.

Sew centered on bunnies back between 4-5 round (counting from the bottom)

Flower

Colour of your choice
R1: sc5 in magic ring, sl st last to first st
R2: *ch3, sl st to next st* repeat for all 5 petals.

End with slip stitch to the back loop of slip stitch made before starting this round.
Fasten off leaving tail for sewing the flower on bunnies body.

Vicky the Bunny

by Teerapon Chan-lam (Jenny)
www.jennyandteddy.com

Skill level:

EASY

Size:

Vicky the Bunny is 5" tall (13 cm).
The doll will work out fine with different crochet hooks: the size of the doll will differ slightly.

Materials:

1. Gray, blue, pink, green and red acrylic yarn. You can use 8 ply yarn.
2. Plastic eyes with safety backing: 7.5mm
3. Fiberfill for stuffing
4. Sewing pins
5. Embroidery thread and needle
6. Optional ribbon
7. Crochet hook size: 1.25mm
8. Craft glue

2 FINE

Abbreviations:

You will need to know how to make a magic ring or adjustable ring.

mr	= magic ring
sc	= single crochet
ch	= chain
inc 1	= increase 1 (2 sc in next st)
dec 1	= decrease 1 (join 2 sts into 1)
sl st	= slip stitch
* * around	= repeat steps
( )	= total no. of sts in a round/row
R	= Round

In this pattern, you will be working in the round continuously. You may use a short contrasting colour piece of yarn to mark the beginning of each round. When you end a round, do not join at the end of each round; you will begin the second round in the next stitch.
At the end of each round, I have given the number of stitches you should have. If you are off by 1 or 2 stitches, do not worry about it.

Head

In grey. Working from top to bottom.

R1: MR and 7sc in ring (7)
R2: 2sc in each st around (14)
R3: *sc in next st, 2sc in next st* repeat around (21)
R4: *sc in next 2 st, 2sc in next st* around (28)
R5: *sc in next 3 st, 2sc in next st* around (35)
R6-13: sc in each st around (35)
R14: *sc in each of next 3 st, dec 1* around (28)
R15: *sc in each of next 2 st, dec 1* around (21)
R16: *sc in each of next st, dec 1* around (14)

Finish off. Leave long end for sewing.
Stuff firmly with polyester.

Body

With blue. Working from bottom to top.

R1: MR and 6sc in ring (6)
R2: 2sc in each st around (12)
R3: *sc in next st, 2sc in next st* around (18)
R4: *sc in next 2 st, 2sc in next st* around (24)
R5: *sc in next 3 st, 2sc in next st* around (30)
R6: sc in each st around (30)
R7: Working in back loops only of round 6, sc in
  each st around (30)

For Skirt
R7.1: Working in front loops only of round 6, Sc in
  each st around (30)
R7.2: Working in front loops only of round 7.1, Sc in
  each st around (30)

Changing to red.
R7.3: Working in front loops only of round 7.2,
  with red: Sc in each st around (30)

Changing to blue.
R8: *sc in each of next 6 st, dec 1* around, after that
  there are 6 st left: make sc in each of those (27)
R9: *sc in each of next 5 st,dec 1* around, after that
  there are 6 st left: make sc in each of that st (24)

Changing to pink.
R10-11: sc in each st around (24)

Changing to blue.
R12: *sc in each of next 4 st, dec 1* around (20)
R13: sc in each st around (20)
R14: *sc in each of next 3 st, dec 1* around (16)
R15: *sc in each of next 2 st, dec 1* around (12)

Finish off. Leave long end for sewing.
Stuff with polyester firmly.

Nose

Make 1 *with white.*

Start with chain 4 (4)

Diagram of round 1:

1sc in st	1sc in st	1sc in st
↓	↓	↓
①	② ③	④
	↑	↑ ↑
	1sc in st	1sc in st 1sc in st

R1: *sc in next 3st from hook* around (6)

R2: *sc in next st, 2sc in next st* around (9)

R3: sc in each of st around (9)

Finish off. Leave long end for sewing. Do not stuff with polyester.

Arms

Make 2. Working from bottom to top.

With grey.

R1: MR and 8sc in ring (8)

R2-8: sc in each st around (8)

Changing to blue.

R9-11: sc in each st around (8)

Finish off. Leave long end for sewing. Stuff a little with polyester.

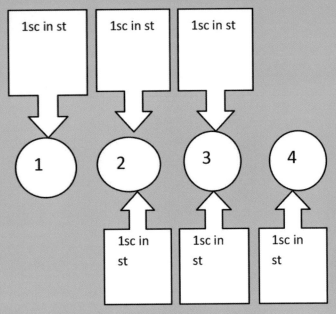

Ears

Make 2 *with grey.*

R1: MR and 5sc in ring (5)

R2: 2sc in each st around (10)

R3: *sc in next st, 2sc in next st* around (15)

R4-5: sc in each st around (15)

R6: *sc in next 2 st, 2sc in next st* around (20)

R7: sc in each st around (20)

R8: *sc in each of next 2 st, dec 1* around (15)

R9: sc in each st around (15)

R10: *sc in next st, dec 1* around (10)

R11-14: sc in each st around (10)

Finish off. Leave long end for sewing and do not stuff with polyester.

Leg

Make 2 *with grey.*

R1: MR and 10sc in ring (10)

R2-8: sc in each st around (10)

Finish off. Leave long end for sewing.

Apple

With red and working from bottom to top.

R1: MR and 6sc in ring (6)
R2: 2sc in each st around (12)
R3: *sc in next st, 2sc in next st* around (18)
R4-6: sc in each st around (18)
R7: *sc in each of next 2 st, dec 1* around. Have last
    2 st free and make sc on each of that st (14)
R8: dec 1 and around until hole is closed.
Finish off. Leave long end for sewing.

Apple Leaf

With green. Start with 30 chains.
Finish off. Leave long tail for sewing.

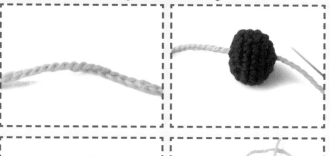

Finishing

Sew ears to the head and finish the face.

Sew body to the head.

Then sew arms and attach legs to body, so that the
bunny is in a standing position.
Note: use pins to adjust and fix position of arms and
legs before sewing.

Helicopter

by Viktorija Dineikiené
www.facebook.com/LovelyBabyGift
www.ravelry.com/designers/lovelybabygift

Skill level:

EASY

Size:

Height: about 3.1 inch (8 cm), **length:** about 5.5 inch (14 cm), **width:** about 2.8 inch (7 cm) (When done with sport weight yarn.)

Note: The size of the helicopter may vary depending on the size of hook and yarn you use.

Materials:

1. Crochet hook (2.75mm; US size C).
2. Sewing needle
3. Blue color yarn: approx. 88 yds (80m)
4. White color yarn: approx. 46 yds (42m)
5. Red color yarn: approx. 22 yds (20m)
6. Black color yarn for eyes and rotor: approx. 1.1 yds (1m)
7. Grey color yarn for eyes: approx. 1.1 yds (1m)
8. Stuffing

The helicopter in the photos was made with sport weight yarn. You can also use worsted weight yarn and a bigger hook.

2 FINE

Abbreviations:

sc = single crochet
ch = chain stitch
st/sts = stitch/stitches
sl st = slip stitch
inc = increase: 2 sc into 1 st
dec = decrease: 1 sc over 2 sts
    (I recommend using invisible decrease)
* * = repeat stitches from * to end of *
O = total number of stitches in a round
R = Round

- I worked in continuous rounds. You may use a stitch marker to mark beginning of rounds.
- The number at the end of each round is the total number of stitches in a round.
- When a number is followed by st, that stitch needs to be worked over that number of stitches.
  Examples:
  5sc means 1sc in each of next 5 stitches;
  Dec 2 times means to decrease 2 times over the next 4sc;
  Inc 5 times means increase in each of next 5 stitches.
- When you see * *, work everything in them as a set.
  Example:
  5sc, dec 2 times, means repeat everything in between the asterisks 2 times.
- Each step is separated by a comma.

30

Body

White color yarn: ch 5

R1: 1sc in 2nd ch from hook, 2sc, 3sc in last st, working across opposite side 2sc, 2sc in last st; (10)

R2: inc, 2sc, inc 3 times, 2sc, inc 2 times; (16)

R3: inc, 4sc, inc 4 times, 4sc, inc 3 times; (24)

R4: *3sc, inc* 6 times; (30)

Sl st in next 6sc (next sc will be the beginning of the next round, move stitch marker);

Red color yarn:

R5-6: sc around; (30)

Blue color yarn:

R7: sc around; (30)

R8: *4sc, inc* 6 times; (36)

Sl st in next sc (next sc will be the beginning of the next round, move stitch marker);

R9: sc around; (36)

Red color yarn:

R10: sc around; (36)

Blue color yarn:

R11: 13sc, sl st in next 10sc, 13sc; (36)

R12: 13sc, inc 10 times, 13sc; (46)

R13: sc around; (46)

R14: 18sc, inc, 8sc, inc, 18sc; (48)

R15: 22sc, inc, 2sc, inc, 22sc; (50)

R16-19: sc around; (50)

Picture after round 17:

Sl st in next 3sc (next sc will be the beginning of the next round, move stitch marker);

R20: 13sc, dec, *5sc, dec* 3 times, 14sc; (46)

R21: sc around; (46)

R22: 14sc, dec, *3sc, dec* 3 times, 15sc; (42)

R23: sc around; (42)

R24: *dec, 5sc* 6 times; (36)

R25: sc around; (36)

R26: *dec, 4sc* 6 times; (30)

R27: sc around; (30)

R28: *dec, 3sc* 6 times; (24)

Start to stuff the body.

R29-30: sc around; (24)

R31: 11sc, inc 4 times, 9sc; (28)

R32: 14sc, inc 2 times, 12sc; (30)

R33: sc around; (30)

R34: 15sc, inc 3 times, 12sc; (33)

R35: sc around; (33)

R36: *dec, 1sc* 11 times; (22)

R37: dec 11 times; (11)

Finish and sew the hole shut.

Eyes

Black color yarn: ch 9
R1: 1sc in 2nd ch from hook, 6sc, 3sc in last st, working across opposite side 6sc, 2sc in last st; (18)

Grey color yarn:
R2: inc, 6sc, inc 3 times, 6sc, inc 2 times; (24)

White color yarn:
R3-5: sc around; (24)

Finish. Leave long end to sew eyes to the body.

Eyelid

Red color yarn: ch 21
R1: 1sc in 2nd ch from hook, 18sc, 3sc in last st, working across opposite side 18sc, 2sc in last st; (42).

Finish and leave long end to sew eyelid onto the eyes.

Rotor blade

(make 4)

Rotor blade has to be filled with stuffing while you`re crocheting it. Stuff the blade lightly.

Blue color yarn: ch 2
R1: 5sc in 2nd ch from hook; (5)
R2: inc 5 times; (10)
R3-7: sc around; (10)

Red color yarn:
R8-9: sc around; (10)

White color yarn:
R10-13: sc around; (10)
R14: *dec, 3sc* 2 times; (8)
R15: *dec, 2sc* 2 times; (6)

Finish, sew the hole shut. Leave long end to sew rotor blade to the body. Make four rotor blades.

Rotor

Black color yarn: ch 2
R1: 5sc in 2nd ch from hook; (5)
R2: inc 5 times; (10)
R3-4: sc around; (10)

Leave long end to sew rotor to the rotor blades.

Skids

(make 2)

Skid has to be filled with stuffing while you`re crocheting it. Stuff the skid lightly.

White color yarn: ch 2
R1: 5sc in 2nd ch from hook; (5)
R2: inc 5 times; (10)
R3-13: sc around; (10)
R14: dec 5 times; (5)

Finish, sew the hole shut. Leave long end to sew skids to the body. Make two skids.

Finishing details

Stuff eyes and sew them to the body:

Separate eyes by sewing blue color yarn in the middle.

Embroider eyes with white yarn.

Sew eyelid onto the eyes.

Embroider mouth area with black yarn (if you prefer, mark mouth area with a textile marker before embroidering).

Sew skids to the body.

Sew rotor blades to the body.

Sew rotor to the rotor blades.

Enjoy!

Lil' Spanish Wedding Dolls

"Don't you just love the classy red gown and penguin suit?

These Spanish Wedding Dolls will make a very special and meaningful gift for you and your loved ones to remember this momentous occasion."

by Rachel Hoe

Little Yarn Friends
www.littleyarnfriends.com

Skill level:

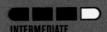

INTERMEDIATE

Materials:

1. Yarn – 8ply acrylic yarn in beige, red, brown, pink, black, white and grey.
2. 3.0 mm crochet hook
3. Yarn needle
4. Tapestry needle
5. Black and white tapestry thread
6. Fiberfill, or any stuffing of your choice
7. 2 pairs of 11.5 mm safety eyes
8. Scissors
9. Stitch marker or safety pin
10. Pink fabric marker or pink cosmetic blusher

Size:

The bride is approximately 18 cm tall and the groom is approximately 20 cm tall. (Sizes may vary depending on the yarn you use and the tension of your stitches.)

Abbreviations:

mr	= magic ring
sc	= single crochet
hdc	= half double crochet
dc	= double crochet
ch	= chain
inc 1	= increase 1 (2 sc in next st)
dec 1	= decrease 1 (join 2 sts into 1)
* * around	= repeat steps
( )	= total no. of sts in a round/row
( )	= different type of sts in 1 st
R	= Round

p.s. All patterns use US crochet terms.

Gauge is not important. (just keep a consistent tension throughout the entire project)
The pattern works in continuous rounds (instead of joined rounds). Except for the bride's skirt layering, flower on head, flower, flower stalk, the groom's bow tie and tuxedo coat.
The Magic Ring is used at the start of most pieces. Alternative technique:
ch 2 and sc 6 into 2nd ch from hook.
You can use Moda Vera 100% acrylic yarn.

Bride
Head & body

With beige and red yarn.
Starting with beige yarn.

R1: MR, sc 6 in MR. (6)
R2: 2 sc in each sc around. (12)
R3: *sc 1, inc 1*, repeat around. (18)
R4: *sc 2, inc 1*, repeat around. (24)
R5: *sc 3, inc 1*, repeat around. (30)
R6: *sc 4, inc 1*, repeat around. (36)
R7: *inc 1, sc 5*, repeat around. (42)
R8: *inc 1, sc 6*, repeat around. (48)
R9: *inc 1, sc 7*, repeat around. (54)
R10-19: sc around. (54)
R20: *dec 1, sc 7*, repeat around. (48)
R21: *dec 1, sc 6*, repeat around. (42)
R22: *dec 1, sc 5*, repeat around. (36)
R23: *dec 1, sc 4*, repeat around. (30)
R24: *dec 1, sc 3*, repeat around. (24)
R25: *dec 1, sc 2*, repeat around. (18)
R26: sc around. (18) - This is the neck.

Insert safety eyes in between round 14 & 15, roughly 10 sts apart. Stuff face with fiberfill.

Change to red yarn.

R27: sc around. (18)
R28: *sc 2, inc 1*, repeat around. (24)
R29: *sc 3, inc 1*, repeat around. (30)
R30: sc around. (30)
R31: *sc 4, inc 1*, repeat around. (36)
R32-46: sc around. (36)
R47: *dec 1, sc 4*, repeat around. (30)
R48: *dec 1, sc 3*, repeat around. (24)

Stuff body with fiberfill.

R49: *dec 1, sc 2*, repeat around. (18)
R50: *dec 1, sc 1*, repeat around. (12)
Stuff fiberfill to fill up the remaining body.
R51: dec around. (6)
Fasten off.

Skirt

With red yarn.

Ch 37.

R1: sc around. (36) – sl st onto the 1st ch, so it becomes a joined round.
R2: hdc around. (36)
R3: *hdc 5, 2 hdc*, repeat around. (42)
R4: *hdc 6, 2 hdc*, repeat around. (48)
R5: *hdc 7, 2 hdc*, repeat around. (54)
R6: *hdc 8, 2 hdc*, repeat around. (60)
R7: *hdc 9, 2 hdc*, repeat around. (66)
R8: *(sc, hdc),(dc, dc),(hdc, sc)*, repeat around. (22 shells)

Sl st, fasten off and weave in the ends.

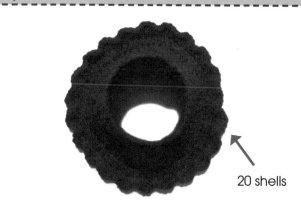

20 shells

Skirt
Lower layer

With red yarn. Working in rows.

Ch 61.

Row 1: sc 2nd ch from hook across. Ch 1 and turn. (60)
Row 2: *(sc, hdc),(dc, dc),(hdc, sc)*, repeat around. (20 shells)

Fasten off.

Skirt
Upper layer

With red yarn. Working in rows.

Ch 49.

Row 1: sc 2nd ch from hook across. Ch 1 and turn. (48)
Row 2: *(sc, hdc),(dc, dc),(hdc, sc)*, repeat around. (16 shells)

Fasten off.

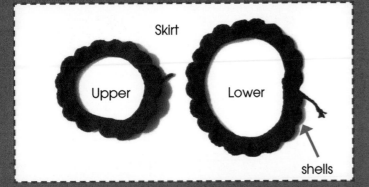

Arms

Make 2 *with beige yarn.*

R1: MR, sc 5 in MR. (5)
R2: *sc 1, inc 1*, repeat around. (7)
R3-15: sc around. (7)
Stuff arms with fiberfill.
R16: dec 3 times, sc 1. (4)
Fasten off.

Sl st, fasten off and weave in the ends

Additional for Plaited Hair:

•   Cut 12 strings of brown yarn, measuring 45cm each.
•   Fold all the strings in half.
•   Use any string to tie a knot in the middle to secure all the strings together.
•   Divide the strings into 3 sections having 8 strings in each section.
•   Plait the strings securely.
•   Once you've plaited to the bottom, use the 2 extreme ends of the strings to go around and tie a knot.
•   Trim the uneven ends at the bottom.

Hair: Side Bun

With brown yarn.
R1: MR, sc 6 in MR. (6)
R2: 2 sc in each sc around. (12)
R3: *sc 1, inc 1*, repeat around. (18)
R4-5: sc around. (18)
R6: *sc 2, dec 1*, repeat 4 times, sc 2. (14)

Hair

With brown yarn.
R1: MR, sc 6 in MR. (6)
R2: 2 sc in each sc around. (12)
R3: *sc 1, inc 1*, repeat around. (18)
R4: *sc 2, inc 1*, repeat around. (24)
R5: *sc 3, inc 1*, repeat around. (30)
R6: *sc 4, inc 1*, repeat around. (36)
R7: *inc 1, sc 5*, repeat around. (42)
R8: *inc 1, sc 6*, repeat around. (48)
R9: *inc 1, sc 7*, repeat around. (54)
R10-18: sc around. (54)

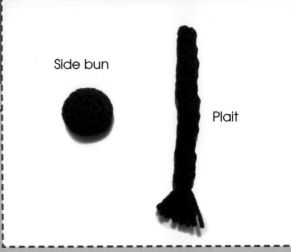

Fasten off.

Flower on Hair

With red yarn.
Ch 19. Starting 2nd ch from hook,
(sc, hdc, dc),(dc, hdc, sc), repeat 9x across.
Fasten off. (9 petals)
Coil it around to make it into a flower shape.

Flower

With pink yarn.
Ch 11. Starting 2nd ch from hook,
(sc, hdc, dc),(dc, hdc, sc), repeat 5x across.
Fasten off. (5 petals)
Coil it around to make it into a flower shape.

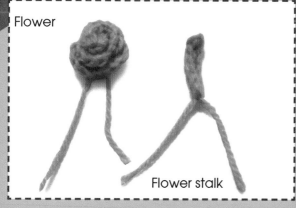

Flower

Flower stalk

Flower stalk

With pink yarn.
Ch 7.
Sc 2nd ch from hook and across the row. (6)
Fasten off.

Assembling the Parts

1. Place the hair onto the bride's head, covering the entire back of the head. Using tapestry needle and black or brown tapestry thread,
- sew the hair onto the head.
- sew the plaited hair across the lower part of main hair piece.
2. Stuff the bottom of the plaited hair into the side bun for a neater look. (Bun placed at the bottom right). Using tapestry needle and black or brown tapestry thread, sew the side bun and stuff fiberfill as you sew.
3. Sew the flower beside the bun.

4. Using tapestry needle and white or red tapestry thread,
- Sew the skirt around Round 33 of the bride's body.
- Sew the lower layer piece to Round 6 of the skirt.
- Sew the upper layer piece to Round 4 of the skirt.

5. Sew the arms on both sides of the bride's body.

6. Sew the flower stalk to the flower. Then sew the flower to the hands.

7. To get rosy cheeks, either use a pink fabric marker or any cosmetic blusher, rub some blusher onto your finger tip and apply it onto both sides of the bride's face.

Groom
Head, body & legs

With beige, white, black and grey yarn.
Starting with beige yarn.
R1: MR, sc 6 in MR. (6)
R2: 2 sc in each sc around. (12)
R3: *sc 1, inc 1*, repeat around. (18)
R4: *sc 2, inc 1*, repeat around. (24)
R5: *sc 3, inc 1*, repeat around. (30)
R6: *sc 4, inc 1*, repeat around. (36)
R7: *inc 1, sc 5*, repeat around. (42)
R8: *inc 1, sc 6*, repeat around. (48)
R9: *inc 1, sc 7*, repeat around. (54)
R10-19: sc around. (54)
R20: *dec 1, sc 7*, repeat around. (48)
R21: *dec 1, sc 6*, repeat around. (42)
R22: *dec 1, sc 5*, repeat around. (36)
R23: *dec 1, sc 4*, repeat around. (30)
R24: *dec 1, sc 3*, repeat around. (24)
R25: *dec 1, sc 2*, repeat around. (18)
R26: sc around. (18) - This is the neck.

Insert safety eyes in between round 14 & 15, roughly 10 sts apart. Stuff face with fiberfill.

Change to white yarn.
R27: sc around. (18)
R28: *sc 2, inc 1*, repeat around. (24)
R29: *sc 3, inc 1*, repeat around. (30)
R30: sc around. (30)
R31: *sc 4, inc 1*, repeat around. (36)
R32-38: sc around. (36)

Change to black yarn.
R39: sc around. (36)

Start of right leg.
R40: sc around 18 times. (18)
Continue on 1st sc on round 40.
R41-48: sc around. (18)
Stuff body and right leg with fiberfill.

Start of the foot.
Stitch marker should be marked on the inner leg.
If it's not, the number of sc may vary before you do
the increase. Gauge accordingly.
R49: sc around front loops only. (18)

Change to grey yarn.
R49: sc around back loops only. (18)
R50: sc 10, inc 6 times, sc 2. (24)
R51-52: sc around. (24)
R53: *sc 2, dec 1*, repeat around. (18)
Stuff fiberfill to remaining part of the foot.
R54: *sc 1, dec 1*, repeat around. (12)
R55: dec around. (6)

Fasten off.

Start of left leg.
Sc direction should start from inner leg and out.
R40: sc around 19 times. (19) Last sc onto the
        inner right leg - crotch area.
Continue on 1st sc on round 40.
R41: sc 17, dec 1. (18)
R42-48: sc around. (18)
Stuff left leg with fiberfill.

Start of the foot.
*Stitch marker should be marked on the inner leg.
If it's not, the number of sc may vary before you
do the increase. Gauge accordingly.*
R49: sc around front loops only. (18)

Change to grey yarn.
R49: sc around back loops only. (18)
R50: sc 2, Inc 6 times, sc 10. (24)
R51-52: sc around. (24)
R53: *sc 2, dec 1*, repeat around. (18)
Stuff fiberfill to remaining part of the foot.
R54: *sc 1, dec 1*, repeat around. (12)
R55: dec around. (6)
Fasten off.

Hair

With brown yarn.
R1: MR, sc 6 in MR. (6)
R2: 2 sc in each sc around. (12)
R3: *sc 1, Inc 1*, repeat around. (18)
R4: *sc 2, Inc 1*, repeat around. (24)
R5: *sc 3, Inc 1*, repeat around. (30)
R6: *sc 4, Inc 1*, repeat around. (36)
R7: *inc 1, sc 5*, repeat around. (42)
R8: *inc 1, sc 6*, repeat around. (48)
R9: *inc 1, sc 7*, repeat around. (54)
R10-19: sc around. (54)

Additional fringe.
R20: sc 1, hdc 1, dc 6. Fasten off.
Attach new yarn. sc 1, hdc 1, dc 4.
Fasten off and weave in the ends.

Bow tie

With grey yarn. Working in rows.
Ch 7
Row1: sc into 2nd ch from hook and across the row,
    ch 1 and turn. (6)
Row2: sc across, ch 1 and turn. (6)
Row3: sc across. (6)
Sc around the edges and fasten off.

Tuxedo Coat

With black yarn. Working in rows.
Ch 21.
Row 1: sc in 2nd ch from hook across (20)
Ch additional 5, turn (24)
Row 2: sc across, ch additional 5, turn (28)
Row 3-13: sc across, ch 1 and turn. (28)

Start of side 1.
Row 14: sc 7, ch 1 and turn. (7)
Row 15: dec 1, sc 3, dec 1, ch 1 and turn. (5)
Row 16: dec 1, sc 1, dec 1, ch 1 and turn. (3)
Row 17: dec 1, sc 1, ch 1 and turn. (2)
Row 18: dec 1. (1)
Fasten off.

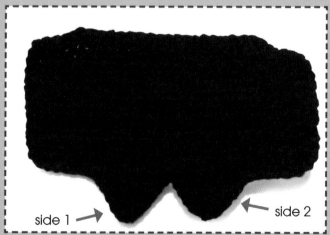

side 1 → ← side 2

Start of side 2. Attach a new piece of yarn.
Row 14: sc 7, ch 1 and turn. (7)
Row 15: dec 1, sc 3, dec 1, ch 1 and turn. (5)
Row 16: dec 1, sc 1, dec 1, ch 1 and turn. (3)
Row 17: dec 1, sc 1, ch 1 and turn. (2)
Row 18: dec 1. (1)
Sc around the edges and fasten off.

Arms

Make 2 with beige and black yarn.
Starting with beige.
R1: MR, sc 6 in MR. (6)
R2: *sc 1, inc 1*, repeat around. (9)
R3-4: sc around. (9)
Change to black yarn.
R5-16: sc around. (9)
Stuff arms with fiberfill.
R17: dec 4 times, sc 1. (5)
Fasten off.

Assembling the Parts

1. Place the hair onto the groom's head, covering the entire back of the head. Using tapestry needle and black or brown tapestry thread, sew the hair onto the head.

2. Using a tapestry needle and black tapestry thread, sew the edges of tuxedo coat to the groom's body. Bend a triangular collar on both side of the coat. Take Row 32 of groom's body as the folding point and continue sewing.

3. Using a tapestry needle and black tapestry thread, sew the arms on both sides of the groom's body.

4. Using a tapestry needle and white or grey tapestry thread, sew the bow tie.

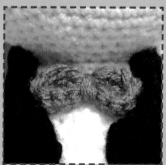

Mia, the Monster Girl

"I learned how to crochet in school, but fell in love with drawing instead. I discovered Amigurumi over 40 years later. As you can see: It's never too late to try something new. My first design was a frog and it started with much trial and error. Nevertheless I was so happy and had to share this joy with a lot of people. You can find a lot of free patterns on my blog: amilovesgurumi.com. I wish you a lot of fun crocheting your little monster girl: Mia."

by Karin Godinez
Soufli, eastern Greece
amilovesgurumi.com

Skill level:

EXPERIENCED

Materials:

1. Crochet hook 2.5 mm
2. Wool: Catania from Schachenmayr: anise (0245), fuchsia (0128)
3. A small amount of wool for the flower: white (0106) and canary (0208)
4. A small amount of pink wool to embroider the mouth
5. Polyester fiberfill
6. 2 pairs of 12 mm/ 0.47 inch safety eyes
7. Tapestry needle, sewing needle

Size:

Mia is 9 inches (23 cm) tall

Abbreviations:

ch = chain
st = stitch
sc = single crochet
inc = increase: make two single crochet in one stitch
dec = decrease: two stitches crochet together with a sc
dcinc = two double crochet in one stitch
sl st = slip stitch
* * repeat = repeat stitches from * to end of *

x = how many times you make a single crochet (or a dc) in each stitch
( ) = total number of stitches in a round/row
R = Round
sc with color change = change the color on this sc (When you make this single crochet stitch, grab the new color of your wool and pull it through the two loops on your hook).

Unless indicated otherwise, the parts for Mia are worked in rounds. You can start with 2 x ch or make a magic ring. Make the fingers with the arms before you start with the legs, because they are crocheted to the body. The rows should be marked with a thread.
Attention: Don't remove the thread marks on the legs and arms, you need them for orientation.

Finger

(3 x for one hand)
2 x ch *with anise*
R1–R5: 6 x sc

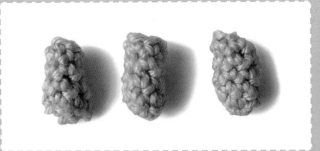

Cut the thread and sew it or tie the two yarn ends together and stuff them into the finger.

Hand with Arm
Make 2

R1: Picture a: Crochet 3 x sc into the first finger, then go ahead and make 3 x sc into the second finger

Picture b: then crochet 6 x sc around the third finger

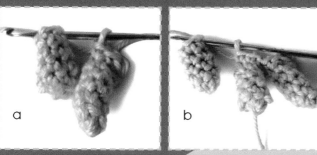

Picture c: finish this round and crochet 3 x sc on the second finger and 3 x sc on the first finger, insert a thread mark for the rounds. (18)

Picture d: You can see how the fingers should look like after the first row.

R2-3: sc in each st around (18)
R4: 9 x sc, dec, 7 x sc (17)
R5: dec, 15 x sc, stuff the fingers (16)
R6: *dec, 2 x sc* repeat 4 times (12)
R7: *dec, 4 x sc* repeat 2 times (10)
R8: sc in each st around, stuff the hand (10)
R9-13: sc in each st around (10)
R14: 5 x sc, inc, 4 x sc (11)
R15-20: sc in each st around (11)
sl st, cut the thread and sew it. Don't stuff the arms.

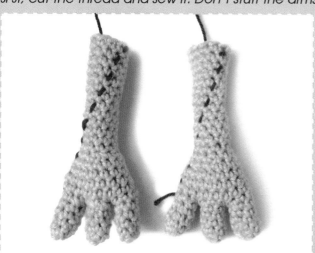

Important: Don't remove the thread marks on the arms, you need them for orientation when you crochet them to the body.

Legs
2 x ch *with anise*

R1: 6 x sc (6)
R2: inc in each st around (12)
R3: *sc, inc* repeat 6 times (18)
R4: *2 x sc, inc* repeat 6 times (24)
R5: *sc, inc* repeat 6 times, 12 x sc (30)
R6: In back loops only : 30 x sc (30)
R7: sc in each st around (30)
R8: *sc, dec* repeat 6 times, 12 x sc (24)
R9: *sc, dec* repeat 4 times, 12 x sc (20)
R10: 2 x sc, dec, sc, dec, sc, dec, 10 x sc (17)
R11-16: sc in each st around (17)
sl st, cut the thread. Don't remove the thread marks on the legs.

Body and Head
With anise

The legs are going to be connected to each other with a sl st, see picture below.

Orientation: Hold legs together with upper inner thighs and toes pointed forward.

Second leg: insert your hook into the second sc before the thread mark.

First leg: Count back 7 stitches from the thread mark and connect both legs.

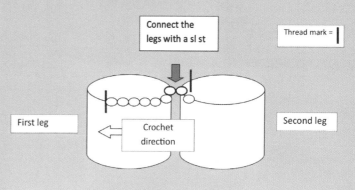

Connect the legs with a sl st

Thread mark = |

First leg

Crochet direction

Second leg

R1: Start in the first leg in the same stitch where you crocheted the sl st: 17 x sc, change to the second leg (make the first stitch in this leg also where you have made the sl st), 17 x sc (34)
Insert a new thread mark for the rounds.
R2: 8 x sc, inc, 16 x sc, inc, 8 x sc (36)
R3: *inc, 5 x sc* repeat 6 times (42)
R4: sc in each st around, stuff the legs (42)
R5: *inc, 6 x sc* repeat 6 times (48)
R6: sc in each st around (48)
R7: sc, inc, *7 x sc, inc* repeat 5 times , 6 x sc (54)
R8-11: sc in each st around (54)
R12: *7 x sc, dec* repeat 6 times (48)
R13-14: sc in each st around (48)
R15: *6 x sc, dec* repeat 6 times (42)
R16-17: sc in each st around (42)
R18: *5 x sc, dec* repeat 6 times (36)
R19: sc in each st around (36)
R20: *7 x sc, dec* repeat 4 times (32)
R21: sc in each st around (32)
R22: *6 x sc, dec* repeat 4 times (28)
R23: sc in each st around (28)
In the next round the arms are crocheted to the body.

Important:
When you connect the arms to the body, make sure that the palm is facing towards the body.

R24: 11 x sc on the body, then crochet with 3 x sc arm and body together, 11 x sc on the body, then crochet the second arm to the body with 3 x sc (28)

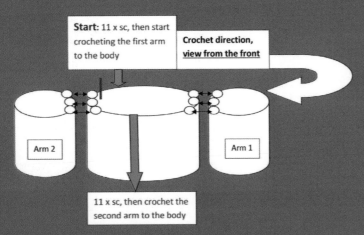

Start: 11 x sc, then start crocheting the first arm to the body

Crochet direction, view from the front

Arm 2
Arm 1

11 x sc, then crochet the second arm to the body

This is how you crochet the first arm to the body.

...and then the second arm.

R25: 11 x sc, then crochet only over the stitches on the arm 8 x sc, 11 x sc on the body and again only over the arm 8 x sc (38)

Picture left: This is the body after R 25, the arrows shows where you have crocheted over the arms. Continue crocheting the rounds on the outside.

R26-27: sc in each st around (38)
R28: 17 x sc, dec, 14 x sc, dec, 3 x sc (36)
R29: *4 x sc, dec* repeat 6 times, stuff the body (30)
R30: dec, 9 x sc, 3 x dec, 9 x sc, 2 x dec (24)
R31: *2 x sc, dec* repeat 6 times (18)
R32-33: sc in each st around (18)
R34: sc in each st around, stuff the body and stuff the shoulders firmly! (18)
R35: inc in each st around (36)
R36: *5 x sc, inc* repeat 6 times (42)
R37: 3 x sc, inc, *6 x sc, inc* repeat 5 times, 3 x sc (48)
R38: *7 x sc, inc* repeat 6 times (54)
R39: 4 x sc, inc, *8 x sc, inc* repeat 5 times, 4 x sc (60)
R40-44: sc in each st around (60)
R45: 49 x sc, 2 x dcinc, 9 x sc (62)

The 2 x dcinc is Mia's nose. If your stitch is not exactly in the center, you may need to add or remove a stitch and do the same number of stitches (plus 1) in R47 until you reach the 2 x dec.

R46: sc in each st around (62)
R47: 50 x sc, 2 x dec, 8 x sc (60)
R48: 44 x sc, put in a thread mark for the position of the first safety eye, 12 x sc, put in a thread mark for the second eye, 4 x sc (60)
R49: *8 x sc, dec* repeat 6 times (54)
R50-53: sc in each st around (54)
R54: *7 x sc, dec* repeat 6 times (48)
R55-56: sc in each st around (48)
R57: *6 x sc, dec* repeat 6 times (42)
R58: 3 x sc, dec, *5 x sc, dec* repeat 5 times, 2 x sc, now put in your safety eyes where you marked the position on R 48 with thread marks (36)
R59: *4 x sc, dec* repeat 6 times, stuff the neck firmly (30)
R60: 2 x sc, dec, *3 x sc, dec* repeat 5 times, sc, stuff the head (24)
R61: sc, dec, *2 x sc, dec* repeat 5 times, sc (18)
R62: *dec, sc* repeat 6 times, Check the head one more time, maybe you have to put in a little bit more fiberfill (12)
R63: 6 x dec (6).
Sl st, cut the thread and sew it

Ears 2 x ch *with anise*
R1: 6 x sc (6)
R2: inc in each st around (12)
R3: *sc, inc* repeat 6 times (18)
R4: *2 x sc, inc* repeat 6 times (24)
R5-8: sc in each st around (24)
R9: fold the ear, then crochet 1 x ch and close the opening with 6 x dec. See pictures on next page (6)

sl st, cut the thread and sew it

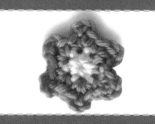

Cut the thread and sew it.

Wig

13 x ch *with fuchsia*
R1: inc in the second ch from hook and work around the chain (top), 10 x sc, 3 x sc in one stitch, continue working on the other side of the chain (bottom): 11 x sc (26)
R2: 2 x inc, 10 x sc, 3 x inc, 10 x sc, inc (32)
R3: *sc, inc* repeat 2 times, 10 x sc, *sc, inc* repeat 3 times, 11 x sc, inc (38)
R4: *inc, 2 x sc* 2 times, 10 x sc, *inc, 2 x sc* 3 times, 10 x sc, inc, 2 x sc (44)
R5: *3 x sc, inc* 2 times, 10 x sc, *3 x sc, inc* 3 times, 13 x sc, inc (50)
R6: *inc, 4 x sc* 2 times, 10 x sc, *inc, 4 x sc* 3 times, 10 x sc, inc, 4 x sc (56)
R7-8: sc in each st around (56)
R9: 18 x sc, dec, 26 x sc, dec, 8 x sc (54)
R10-11: sc in each st around (54)
Cut the thread & sew it.

Hair

Start in the first stitch after the thread mark.
Tip: Crochet the 1st ch with two threads & continue with one thread, so the chain cannot dissolve.

Make chains in every stitch around the wig and cut the thread after every chain.
11 chains with each 32 x ch, 10 chains with each 28 x ch, 4 chains with each 26 x ch,
2 chains with each 24 x ch, 10 chains with each 22 x ch, 2 chains with each 24 x ch,
4 chains with each 26 x ch, 10 chains with each 28 x ch, 1 chain with 32 x ch.

Flower for the hair

2 x ch with white
R1: 5 x sc, sc with *color change to canary* (6)
R2: sc, 3 x ch, sc in the same stitch, *sc in next stitch, 3 x ch, sc in the same stitch* repeat 5 times.

Finishing

Pin the ears to the head and sew them.

Pin the wig to the head and sew it.

Take 9 strands of the hair and sew the flower to the hair and to the head

Shaping the belly button: Insert your needle with anise wool from the back and pull it to the front, leave a long tail in the back.
Then skip three stitches and pull the needle to the back again. **Important:** The needle has to be in the same stitch, where you started from.

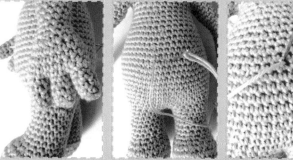

Pull the thread so it forms a belly button in the front and make a knot in the back with the two strands and hide them inside the body.
Embroider a mouth with pink wool and Mia, your monster girl is finished!

43

Lil' Valentine's Teddy

Isn't he adorable? Teddies are versatile gifts for all occasions.
To add to his cuteness, Teddy has a heart shape sewn onto his back.

by Rachel Hoe
Little Yarn Friends, www.littleyarnfriends.com

Skill level:

EASY

2 FINE

Materials:

1. Yarn – 8ply acrylic yarn in light brown, small amount of black and red
2. 3.0mm crochet hook
3. Yarn needle
4. Tapestry needle
5. White/light brown tapestry thread
6. Fiberfill or any stuffing of your choice
7. 1 pair of 4mm beads
8. Scissors
9. Stitch marker or safety pin

Size:

The teddy is approximately 13cm x 11cm (5.1" x 4.3"). (In sitting position.)

Abbreviations:

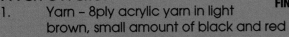

MR   = magic ring
sc   = single crochet
hdc   = half double crochet
dc   = double crochet
ch   = chain
inc 1   = increase 1 (2 sc in next st)
dec 1   = decrease 1 (join 2 sts into 1)
sl st   = slip stitch
* *   = repeat step
( )   = total no. of sts in a round
R   = round

This pattern is written using US crochet terms.
Gauge is not important. Just keep a consistent tension throughout the entire project.

This pattern is worked in continuous rounds (instead of joined rounds).
The Magic Ring is used at the start of all pieces.
Alternative technique: ch 2 and sc 6 into 2nd ch from hook.

Head & Body

With light brown yarn.
R1: MR, sc 6 in MR. (6)
R2: 2 sc in each sc around. (12)
R3: *sc 1, inc 1*, repeat around. (18)
R4: *sc 2, inc 1*, repeat around. (24)
R5: *sc 3, inc 1*, repeat around. (30)
R6: *sc 4, inc 1*, repeat around. (36)
R7: *inc 1, sc 5*, repeat around. (42)
R8: *inc 1, sc 6*, repeat around. (48)
R9-17: sc around. (48)
R18: *dec 1, sc 6*, repeat around. (42)
R19: *dec 1, sc 5*, repeat around. (36)
R20: *dec 1, sc 4*, repeat around. (30)
R21: *dec 1, sc 3*, repeat around. (24)
R22: *dec 1, sc 2*, repeat around. (18)
R23: sc around. (18) - This is the neck.

Stuff head with fiberfill.

R24: *sc 2, inc 1*, repeat around. (24)
R25: *sc 3, inc 1*, repeat around. (30)
R26: sc around. (30)
R27: *sc 4, inc 1*, repeat around. (36)
R28-31: sc around. (36)
R32: *dec 1, sc 4*, repeat around. (30)
R33: *dec 1, sc 3*, repeat around. (24)

Stuff body with fiberfill.

R34: *dec 1, sc 2*, repeat around. (18)
R35: *dec 1, sc 1*, repeat around. (12)

Stuff fiberfill to fill up the remaining body.
R36: dec around. (6)
Fasten off.

Ears

Make 2 with light brown yarn.
R1: MR, sc 6 in MR. (6)
R2: 2 sc in each sc around. (12)
R3: *sc 1, inc 1*, repeat around. (18)
R4-5: sc around. (18)
Fasten off and leave a long end to attach to the head.
Flatten. Do not stuff with fiberfill.

Snout

With light brown yarn.
R1: MR, sc 6 in MR. (6)
R2: 2 sc in each sc around. (12)
R3: *sc 1, inc 1*, repeat around. (18)
R4: *sc 2, inc 1*, repeat around. (24)
R5-6: sc around. (24)
Fasten off and leave a long end to attach to the face.

Nose

With black yarn.
R1: MR, sc 6 in MR. (6)
R2: 2 sc in each sc around. (12)
R3: *dec 1, sc 1*, repeat around. (8)
Stuff nose with fiberfill.
Fasten off and leave a long end to attach to the snout.

Arms

Make 2 with light brown
R1: MR, sc 6 in MR. (6)
R2: 2 sc in each sc around. (12)
R3-11: sc around. (12)
Stuff arm with fiberfill.
R12: dec around. (6)
Fasten off.

Legs

Make 2 with light brown yarn
R1: MR, sc 6 in MR. (6)
R2: 2 sc in each sc around. (12)
R3: *sc 1, inc 1*, repeat around. (18)
R4: *sc 2, inc 1*, repeat around. (24)
R5-7: sc around. (24)
R8: dec 6, sc around. (18)
R9-10: sc around. (18)
R11: *dec 1, sc 1*, repeat around. (12)
R12: sc around. (12)
Stuff leg with fiberfill.
R13: dec 3 only. (6) You won't finish the Round.
Fasten off, leave a long end and weave in and out to close the gap.

Heart on butt

With red yarn.
MR, ch 2.
(Crochet the following sts through the MR)
3 dc, 1 hdc, 1 dc, 1 hdc, 3 dc, ch 2. Sl St through the MR and close the MR.
Fasten off and weave in the end.

Assembling the Parts

(2 ways to attach the pieces together)
- Using a yarn needle and ends from the various parts
OR
- Using a tapestry needle and white/light brown tapestry thread.

1. Sew the ears on both sides after Round 5 counting from the top of the head.

2. Sew the snout after Round 12 of the head. Stuff fiberfill as you sew.

3. Sew the nose after Round 2 of the snout. (placement towards the top of the snout)

4. Sew the arms at the side of the body.

5. Sew legs after Round 5 of the body counting from the bottom.

6. Sew the eyes after Round 11 of the head and 4 stitches apart.

7. Lastly, sew the heart at the teddy's butt area.

Congratulations! You've successfully completed your Lil' Valentine's Teddy!

Mr. Golden Sun

"Oh, Mr. Sun, Sun, Mr. Golden Sun, please shine down on me...
Mr Golden Sun is here to melt your heart and bring you lots of joy.
Hooray for sunny days!!"

by Gemma Cubells
www.tremenducrochet.com

Skill level:

EASY

4 MEDIUM

Materials:

1.   Worsted weight yarn in yellow and dark yellow color
2.   Size G (4 mm) crochet hook
3.   Pink embroidery floss
4.   Small piece of pink craft felt and sewing thread that matches.
5.   Sharp embroidery needle
6.   Tapestry needle
7.   Fiberfill or stuffing of your choice
8.   Stitch marker
9.   10 mm plastic eyes with safety backings

Size:

Mr. Golden Sun is 5,5" tall (14 cm).

Abbreviations:

sc	= single crochet
ch	= chain
dc	= double crochet
hdc	= half double crochet
sl st	= slip stitch
* *	repeat steps
( )	= total no. of sts in a round
st(s)	= stitche(s)
R	= round(s)
( )	= different type of sts in 1 st

Body and Sun Rays

Make 2 using G hook and *light yellow yarn.*
R1: ch 2, 6 sc in second ch from hook.
R2: sc 2 in each sc around. (12)
R3: *sc 1, 2 sc in next sc*, repeat 6 times. (18)
R4: *sc 2, 2 sc in next sc*, repeat 6 times. (24)
R5: *sc 3, 2 sc in next sc*, repeat 6 times. (30)
R6: *sc 4, 2 sc in next sc*, repeat 6 times. (36)
R7: *sc 5, 2 sc in next sc*, repeat 6 times. (42)
R8: *sc 6, 2 sc in next sc*, repeat 6 times. (48)
R9: *sc 7, 2 sc in next sc*, repeat 6 times. (54)
R10: *sc 8, 2 sc in next sc*, repeat 6 times. (60)
R11-R15: sc 60.
Proceed to next round to begin the sun rays.
Change to dark yellow yarn and leave a long tail of light yellow yarn for sewing.

Working into the front loop only.
R16: Sc 60.

Working in both loops,
R17: *Skip 1, 3 hdc in next sc, (dc 1, ch 3, dc 1) in next sc, 3 hdc in next sc, skip 1, sl st 1*, repeat 10 times. *Fasten off, leaving long tail for sewing.*

How to: work into the front loops

1. Look for the V's across the top of the stitches.

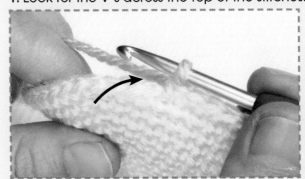

46

2. Insert the hook underneath the front loop of each V.

3. Make a simple crochet. Continue working through the front loop all around body.

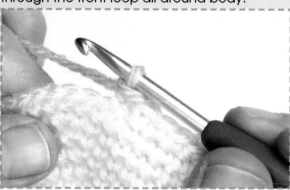

4. You will use the back loops later to join the two parts of the sun body together.

Face

Position and attach eyes, embroider mouth. For cheeks, cut 2 circles from pink felt and sew to face.

Position the two body pieces together with their sun rays and stitches of the last row matching up.

Join the two parts of the sun body together using the back loop you left on round 15 (where you made the color change), stuffing it before you close it.

Join the sun rays together on round 17, using the back loop of every stitch.

How to: join the Sun Rays

1. Thread a yarn needle with the long dark yellow yarn end you left for sewing.

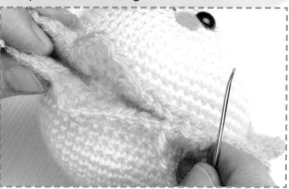

2. Insert the needle through the back loop of the corresponding stitches on both pieces.

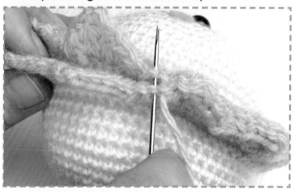

3. Draw the yarn all the way through, but do not pull it overly tight.

4. Repeat steps 2 and 3 for each stitch around the two pieces. Fasten off and weave in ends.

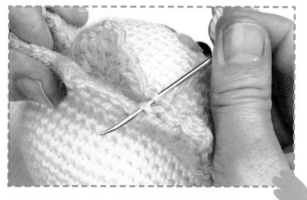

Merry, the Christmas Elf

"Shhh... Have you heard the little noises? He is Merry, the Christmas Elf who brings you presents and joy!
May your days be Merry and bright."

by Gemma Cubells
www.tremenducrochet.com

Skill level:

INTERMEDIATE

Materials:

1. Worsted weight yarn in 4 colors: desired skin color, broken white, red and desired hair color
2. Size G (4 mm) crochet hook
3. Pink embroidery floss
4. Small button
5. Embroidery needle
6. Tapestry needle
7. Fiberfill or stuffing of your choice
8. Stitch marker
9. 13 mm plastic eyes with safety backings

4 MEDIUM

Size:

Merry, the Christmas Elf is 10" tall (25 cm).
The hat is 7.5" long (19 cm).

Abbreviations:

sc = single crochet
ch = chain
dc = double crochet
hdc = half double crochet
tr = triple crochet

dec = single crochet decrease
sl st = slip stitch
* * repeat = repeat steps between asterisks
( ) = total no. of sts in a round
st(s) = stitche(s)
R = round(s)

Arms

Make 2. Using G hook *and skin-colored yarn.*
R1: ch 2, 6 sc in second ch from hook.
R2: sc 2 in each sc around. (12)
R3-R4: sc 12.
R5: *sc 1, dec 1*, repeat 4 times. (8)
R6: sc 8.
Change to red yarn.
R7: sc 8.
Change to broken white yarn.
R8-R9: sc 8.
Slightly stuff hand and continue crocheting.
Change to red yarn.
R10: sc 8.
Change to broken white yarn.
R11-R12: sc 8.

Change to red yarn.
R13: sc 8.
Change to broken white yarn.
R14-R15: sc 8.
Change to red yarn.
R16: sc 8.
Change to broken white yarn.
R17-R18: sc 8.
Change to red yarn.
R19: sc 8.
Change to broken white yarn.
R20: sc 8.

Fasten off, leaving long tail for sewing and set aside.

How to: work into the front loops

All stitches are worked in both loops of the stitches, unless otherwise directed.

1. Look for the V's across the top of the stitches.

2. Insert the hook underneath the front loop of each V and make a simple crochet

3. You will use the back loops later when crocheting the body.

Legs of the pants

Make 2. Starting at bottom of foot, using G hook *and red yarn.*
R1: ch 7, sc 6 starting in second chain from hook, then work 6 sc on opposite side of chain. (12)
R2: 2 sc in first stitch, sc 4, 2 sc in next 2 sts, sc 4, 2 sc in last stitch. (16)
R3: sc 1, 2 sc in next st, sc 5, 2 sc in next st, sc 1, 2 sc in next st, sc 5, sc in last st. (20)
R4: sc 20.
R5: sc 5, dec 2 times, sc 2, dec 2 times, sc 5. (16)
R6: sc 5, dec 3 times, sc 5. (13)
R7: sc 5, dec 1, sc 6. (12)
R8: sc 12.

Stuff foot and continue crocheting.

R9-R17: sc 12.

Stuff leg and continue crocheting.

R18 for left leg: Fasten off, leaving long tail for sewing, and set aside.
R18 for right leg: Sc 6, sc in each st of the last round of the left leg (12 sts), sc 6 (remaining stitches of right leg). (24)

Do not fasten off, proceed to next round to continue with the top of the elf pants.

Top of the Pants

R19: *sc 3, 2 sc in next sc*, repeat 6 times. (30)
R20: *sc 4, 2 sc in next sc*, repeat 6 times. (36)
R21: *sc 5, 2 sc in next sc*, repeat 6 times. (42)
R22: *sc 6, 2 sc in next sc*, repeat 6 times. (48)
R23: *sc 7, 2 sc in next sc*, repeat 6 times. (54)
R24-R26: sc 54.
R27: *sc 7, dec 1*, repeat 6 times. (48)
R28: sc 48.

Working into the front loop only.

R29: sc 12, ch 40, sc in second ch from hook and next 38 ch stitches, sc 36 (remaining stitches of the round). (48)

Fasten off and weave in ends.

How to: join legs

1. Mark you first st with st marker. Sc 6 sts of the leg your yarn is attached to (the right leg of the doll).

2. Sc in each st of the last left leg round, starting into the next st you fasten off the yarn.

3. Sc the remaining 6 sts of the right leg. The legs are now joined. Continue crocheting the next 2 rounds.

4. Attach the hole between legs, with the yarn tail you left on the left leg. (see photo below)

5. This is the result!

How to: join yarn to one of the back loops

1. Make a slip knot and place it on your hook.

2. Insert the hook into the back loop you want to start with.

3. Make a simple crochet.

4. Continue working through the back loop all around body. This is the result!

Body

Using G hook and broken white yarn.
Join yarn to one of the back loops you left in round 29 of the elf pants.
Working through the back loops all around body
R1: sc 48.

Working in both loops.
R2: *sc 6, dec 1*, repeat 6 times. (42)

Change to red yarn.
R3: sc 42.

Change to broken white yarn.
R4: *sc 5, dec 1*, repeat 6 times. (36)
R5: sc 36.

Change to red yarn.
R6: *sc 4, dec 1*, repeat 6 times. (30)

Change to broken white yarn.
R7-R8: sc 30.

Change to red yarn.
R9: sc 30.

Stuff body and continue crocheting.
Change to broken white yarn.
R10: *sc 3, dec 1*, repeat 6 times. (24)
R11: sc 24.

Change to red yarn.
R12: *sc 2, dec 1*, repeat 6 times. (18)

Remove hook, but do not fasten off.
Flatten arms and attach to body at round 10.
Do not fasten off, proceed to next round to begin the head.

Head

Change to skin-colored yarn.
Working into the back loop only.
R13: sc 18.

Working in both loops.
R14: *sc 2, 2 sc in next sc*, repeat 6 times. (24)
R15: *sc 3, 2 sc in next sc*, repeat 6 times. (30)
R16: *sc 4, 2 sc in next sc*, repeat 6 times. (36)
R17: *sc 5, 2 sc in next sc*, repeat 6 times. (42)
R18: *sc 6, 2 sc in next sc*, repeat 6 times. (48)
R19: *sc 7, 2 sc in next sc*, repeat 6 times. (54)
R20: *sc 8, 2 sc in next sc*, repeat 6 times. (60)
R21-R28: sc 60.

Stuff neck firmly and continue crocheting.
R29: *sc 8, dec 1*, repeat 6 times. (54)
R30: *sc 7, dec 1*, repeat 6 times. (48)
R31: *sc 6, dec 1*, repeat 6 times. (42)
R32: *sc 5, dec 1*, repeat 6 times. (36)
R33: *sc 4, dec 1*, repeat 6 times. (30)

Remove hook, but do not fasten off.
Work on face: position and attach eyes, embroider mouth.
Stuff head and continue crocheting.
R34: *sc 3, dec 1*, repeat 6 times. (24)
R35: *sc 2, dec 1*, repeat 6 times. (18)

Stuff a little more and continue crocheting.

R36: *sc 1, dec 1*, repeat 6 times. (12)
R37: *dec 1*, repeat 6 times. (6)
R38: sc next and 4th st together.

Fasten off, pulling knot to center.
Sew pants strap in place, with a button on the strap end.

Hair

Using G hook and hair coloured yarn.
R1: ch 2, 6 sc in second ch from hook.
R2: sc 2 in each sc around. (12)
R3: *sc 1, 2 sc in next sc*, repeat 6 times. (18)
R4: *sc 2, 2 sc in next sc*, repeat 6 times. (24)
R5: *sc 3, 2 sc in next sc*, repeat 6 times. (30)
R6: *sc 4, 2 sc in next sc*, repeat 6 times. (36)
R7: *sc 5, 2 sc in next sc*, repeat 6 times. (42)
R8: *sc 6, 2 sc in next sc*, repeat 6 times. (48)
R9: *sc 7, 2 sc in next sc*, repeat 6 times. (54)
R10: *sc 8, 2 sc in next sc*, repeat 6 times. (60)
R11-R20: sc 60.
R21: hdc 1, dc 1, tr 1, ch 3, turn, dc 1, hdc 1, sc 1, sl st 1, sc 36.

Fasten off, leaving long tail for sewing.
Position and sew the round 19 of the hair to the head.

Elf Hat

Using G hook and red yarn.
R1: ch 2, 6 sc in second ch from hook.
R2: sc 2 in each sc around. (12)
R3-R4: sc 12.
R5: *sc 2, 2 sc in next sc*, repeat 4 times. (16)
R6-R7: sc 16.
R8: *sc 3, 2 sc in next sc*, repeat 4 times. (20)
R9-R10: sc 20.
R11: *sc 4, 2 sc in next sc*, repeat 4 times. (24)
R12-R13: sc 24.
R14: *sc 5, 2 sc in next sc*, repeat 4 times. (28)
R15-R16: sc 28.
R17: *sc 6, 2 sc in next sc*, repeat 4 times. (32)
R18-R19: sc 32.
R20: *sc 7, 2 sc in next sc*, repeat 4 times. (36)
R21-R22: sc 36.
R23: *sc 8, 2 sc in next sc*, repeat 4 times. (40)
R24-R25: sc 40.
R26: *sc 9, 2 sc in next sc*, repeat 4 times. (44)
R27-R28: sc 44.
R29: *sc 10, 2 sc in next sc*, repeat 4 times. (48)
R30-R31: sc 48.
R32: *sc 11, 2 sc in next sc*, repeat 4 times. (52)
R33-R34: sc 52.
R35: *sc 12, 2 sc in next sc*, repeat 4 times. (56)
R36-R37: sc 56.
R38: *sc 13, 2 sc in next sc*, repeat 4 times. (60)
R39-R40: sc 60.

Fasten off and weave in ends.
Optional: make a little pompom using broken white yarn and attach it on top of the elf hat.

Lil' Corgi Puppy

Calling all dog lovers and Corgi lovers! This crochet pattern is for you! Suitable for beginners, this will make a meaningful gift for all dog lovers. This size is suitable to make into a keychain, brooch or simply an adorable display.

by Rachel Hoe
Little Yarn Friends, www.littleyarnfriends.com

Skill level:

EASY

Materials:

1. Yarn – 8ply acrylic yarn in golden brown, white and a little black.
2. 3.00 mm crochet hook
3. Yarn needle
4. Tapestry needle
5. White tapestry thread
6. Fiberfill or any stuffing of your choice
7. 1 pair of 4 mm beads
8. Scissors
9. Stitch marker or safety pin

Size:

Approximately 6cm (8cm with tail) x 7cm. (2.4" x 2.8")

Abbreviations:

MR = magic ring
sc = single crochet
ch = chain
inc 1 = increase 1 (2 sc in next st)
dec 1 = decrease 1 (join 2 sts into 1)
* * = repeat step
( ) = total no. of sts in a round/row

This pattern is written using US crochet terms.
Gauge is not important. (just keep a consistent tension throughout the entire project)
This pattern works in continuous rounds (instead of joined rounds), except for the head parting.
The Magic Ring is used at the start of most pieces. Alternative technique: ch 2 and sc 6 into 2nd ch from hook.
I used Moda Vera 100% acrylic yarn for my corgi puppies.

Head

With golden brown yarn.
R1: MR, sc 6 in MR. (6)
R2: 2 sc in each sc around. (12)
R3: *sc 1, inc 1*, repeat around. (18)
R4: *sc 2, inc 1*, repeat around. (24)
R5-9: sc around. (24)
R10: *dec 1, sc 2*, repeat around. (18)
Stuff head with fiberfill.
R11: *dec 1, sc 1*, repeat around. (12)
Stuff with fiberfill to fill up the remaining head.
R12: dec around. (6)
Fasten off and leave a long end to sew to the body.

Head Parting (white stripe)

With white yarn.
Ch 7.
Fasten off.

Body

White and golden brown yarn.
Start with white yarn.
R1: MR, sc 6 in MR. (6)
R2: 2 sc in each sc around. (12)
R3: sc around. (12)

Change to golden brown yarn.
R4-11: sc around. (12)

Stuff body with fiberfill.
R12: dec around

Fasten off.

Ears

Make 2 with golden brown yarn.
R1: MR, sc 4 in MR. (4)
R2: *sc 1, inc 1*, repeat around. (6)
R3: *sc 2, inc 1*, repeat around. (8)
R4: *sc 3, inc 1*, repeat around. (10)
R5: sc around. (10)

Flatten each ear. Do not stuff fiberfill.

Fasten off and leave a long end to sew to the head.

Snout

White yarn.
R1: MR, sc 6 in MR. (6)
R2: *sc 1, inc 1*, repeat around. (9)
R3-4: sc around. (9)

Fasten off and leave a long end to sew to the head.

Legs

Make 4 with white and golden brown yarn.
Start with white yarn.
R1: MR, sc 4 in MR. (4)
R2: sc around. (4)

Change to golden brown yarn.
R3-4: sc around. (4)

Stuff a bit of fiberfill in each leg.
Fasten off and leave a long end to sew to the body.

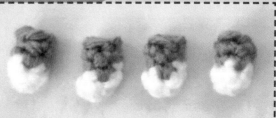

Tail

Golden Brown Yarn.
R1: MR, sc 4 in MR. (4)
R2-5: sc around. (4)

Stuff a bit of fiberfill in the tail.
Fasten off and leave a long end to sew to the body.

Assembling The Parts

1. Using white/matching coloured tapestry thread and tapestry needle, sew the head parting to the head, from top center of the head downwards.

2. Using black yarn and yarn needle, embroider a nose onto the snout. (nose should stop after Round 2 on snout)

3. Using a yarn needle,
- Sew the snout on Round 7 of head.
  Stuff fiberfill as you sew.
- Sew ears on each side after Round 2 on the head.
- Sew the legs onto the bottom part of the body (front legs on Round 3 to Round 5 and back legs on Round 8 to Round 10 of body)
- Sew the tail on Round 11 of body.
- Sew the head to the body. (approximately head placement - Round 3 to Round 6 of body)
- Alternative method: You can use tapestry thread and tapestry needle to sew the parts together.

4. Lastly, using white/matching coloured tapestry thread and tapestry needle sew the eyes onto the face. (approximately 1 to 2 stitches away from the snout)

Bowling Friends

by Karin Godinez
www.amilovesgurumi.com

Skill level:

EASY

Materials:

1. Crochet hook: 2.5 mm
2. Catania wool from Schachenmayr
3. Polyester fiberfill
4. For each pin 2 safety eyes, size 9 mm/ 0.35 inches
5. Tapestry needle, sewing needle

2 FINE

Size:

Each pin is 5.5 inches (14 cm) tall.

Abbreviations:

ch = chain
st = stitch
sc = single crochet
inc = increase: make two single crochet in one stitch
dec = decrease: two stitches crochet together with a sc
sl st = slip stitch
* * repeat = repeat stitches from * to end of *
x = how many times you make a single crochet or a dc in each stitch
( ) = total number of stitches in a round/row
R = round
sc with color change = change the color on this sc (When you make this single crochet stitch, grab the new color of your wool and pull it through the two loops on your hook).

Unless indicated otherwise, the pins are worked in rounds. You can start with 2 x ch or make a magic ring. The rows should be marked with a thread.

Pin

2 x ch with *main color*
R1: 6 x sc (6)
R2: inc in each st around (12)
R3: *sc, inc* repeat 6 times (18)
R4: *2 x sc, inc* repeat 6 times (24)
R5: *3 x sc, inc* repeat 6 times (30)
R6: In back loops only: 30 x sc (30)
R7-8: sc in each st around (30)
R9: sc with color change to **color 1**, 29 x sc (30)
R10: *9 x sc, inc* repeat 3 times (33)
R11: 5 x sc, inc, *10 x sc, inc* repeat 2 times, 5 x sc (36)
R12: sc with color change to **main color**, 35 x sc (36)
R13: *11 x sc, inc* repeat 3 times (39)
R14: sc with color change to **color 2**, 38 x sc (39)
R15-16: sc in each st around (39)
R17: sc with color change to **main color**, 38 x sc (39)
R18: *11 x sc, dec* repeat 3 times (36)
R19: sc with color change to **color 1**, 35 x sc (36)
R20: 5 x sc, dec, *10 x sc, dec* repeat 2 times, 5 x sc (33)
R21: sc in each st around (33)
R22: sc with color change to **main color**, 8 x sc, dec, *9 x sc, dec* repeat 2 times (30)
R23: sc in each st around (30)
R24: 4 x sc, dec, *8 x sc, dec* repeat 2 times, 4 x sc (27)
R25: *7 x sc, dec* repeat 3 times (24)
R26: 3 x sc, dec, *6 x sc, dec* repeat 2 times, 3 x sc (21)
R27: *5 x sc, dec* repeat 3 times, stuff the body (18)
R28-31: sc in each st around (18)
R32: inc in each st around (36)
R33: *5 x sc, inc* repeat 6 times (42)
R34-37: sc in each st around (42)

STRIKE

R38: 28 x sc, put in a thread mark to mark the place for the safety eye, 10 x sc, put in a thread mark for the second safety eye, 4 x sc (42)

R39-42: sc in each st around (42)

R43: *5 x sc, dec* repeat 6 times (36)

R44: 2 x sc, dec, *4 x sc, dec* repeat 5 times, 2 x sc (30), plug in the safety eyes

R45: *3 x sc, dec* repeat 6 times (24) stuff the head

R46: *2 x sc, dec* repeat 6 times (18)

R47: *sc, dec* repeat 6 times (12) stuff the head again before you close it

R48: 6 x dec (6)

sl st, cut the thread and sew it.

Finishing Pin

Starting in the bottom of the pin with **main color**, the head is looking towards you

R1: 30 x sc in the front loops from R 6

R2: 30 x sl st, cut the thread and sew it. See pictures.

Cat

Main color: cream 0130, **color 1:** light pink 0246, **color 2:** lavender 0226

Ears

Make 2. 2 x ch *with **main color***

R1: 6 x sc (6)

R2: *2 x sc, inc* repeat 2 times (8)

R3: *3 x sc, inc* repeat 2 times (10)

R4: *4 x sc, inc* repeat 2 times (12)

R5: *5 x sc, inc* repeat 2 times (14)

R6: *6 x sc, inc* repeat 2 times (16)

sl st, cut the thread and sew the opening, see picture.

Finishing Cat

Embroider the nose and the mouth, pin the ears to the head and sew them.

Frog

Main color: apple green 0205, **color 1 and 2:** cream 0130

The frog has a different head. Crochet the pattern for the pin until row 33 and continue with the pattern for the frog's head.

Head

R34-35: sc in each st around (42)

R36: *6 x sc, inc* repeat 6 times (48)

R37-39: sc in each st around (48)

R40: 3 x sc, dec, *6 x sc, dec* repeat 5 times, 3 x sc (42)

R41: *5 x sc, dec* repeat 6 times (36)

R42: 2 x sc, dec, *4 x sc, dec* repeat 5 times, 2 x sc (30)

R43: *3 x sc, dec* repeat 6 times (24) stuff the head

R44: *2 x sc, dec* repeat 6 times (18)

R45: *sc, dec* repeat 6 times (12) stuff the head again before you close it

R46: 6 x dec (6)

sl st, cut the thread and sew it.

Eyes

2 x ch *with **color 1***

R1: 6 x sc (6)

R2: inc in each st around (12)

R3: *sc, inc* repeat 6 times (18)

R4: *2 x sc, inc* repeat 6 times (24)

R5-6: sc in each st around (24)

R7: *2 x sc, dec* repeat 6 times (18)

Now plug in the safety eyes, where you have started with 2 x ch or a Magic Ring

R8: *sc, dec* repeat 6 times (12) stuff the eye

R9: 6 x dec (6)

sl st, cut the thread and sew it.

STRIKE

55

Finishing frog

Embroider the mouth, pin the eyes to the head and sew them.

Dog

Main color: taupe 0254, **color 1:** flesh 0257, **color 2:** linen 0248, **color 3:** chocolate 0162

Ears

Make 2. 2 x ch *with color 1*

R1: 4 x sc (4)
R2: *inc, sc* repeat 2 times (6)
R3: *inc, 2 x sc* repeat 2 times (8)
R4: *inc, 3 x sc* repeat 2 times (10)
R5-11: sc in each st around (10)

Close the opening with 4 x sc, sl st, *cut the thread and sew it. (see picture)*

Muzzle

2 x ch *with color 1*

R1: 6 x sc (6)
R2: inc in each st around (12)
R3: *3 x sc, 3 x inc* repeat 2 times (18)
R4: 4 x sc, inc, 2 x sc, inc, 5 x sc, inc, 2 x sc, inc, sc (22)
R5-6: sc in each st around (22)
R7: sl st in each st around (22)

Cut the thread and sew it.

Nose

2 x ch *with color 3*

R1: 6 x sc (6)
R2: *inc, 2 x sl st* repeat 2 times (8)

Cut the thread.

Finishing dog

Pin the nose to the muzzle and sew it.
Stuff the muzzle with fiberfill and pin the muzzle and the ears to the head and sew them.

Duck

Main color: canary 0208, **color 1:** natural 0105, **color 2:** orange 0189

Beak

Make 2. 2 x ch *with color 2*

R1: 6 x sc (6)
R2: inc in each st around (12)
R3: *3 x sc, 3 x inc* repeat 2 times (18)
R4: 5 x sc, dec, 7 x sc, dec, 2 x sc (16)
R5: 4 x sc, dec, 6 x sc, dec, 2 x sc (14)
R6: sl st in each st around (14)

Cut the thread and sew it.

Finishing duck

Pin the beaks to the head and sew them.

Cow

Main color: linen 0248, **color 1:** chocolate 0162, **color 2:** light pink 0246, **color 3:** natural 0105

Horns

Make 2. 2 x ch *with color 3*

R1: 6 x sc (6)
R2-4: sc in each st around (6)
R5: sl st in each st around (6)

Cut the thread and sew it.

Ears

Make 2. 2 x ch *with color 1*

R1: 6 x sc (6)
R2: *sc, inc* repeat 3 times (9)
R3: *2 x sc, inc* repeat 3 times (12)
R4: *3 x sc, inc* repeat 3 times (15)
R5: sc in each st around (15)

Close the opening with 7 x sc, sl st, *cut the thread and sew it.*

Then fold the ear one time and sew the ends together, see picture on the right below.

Nose

2 x ch *with color 2*

R1: 6 x sc (6)
R2: inc in each st around (12)

R3: *3 x sc, 3 x inc* repeat 2 times (18)
R4: 3 x sc,*inc, sc* repeat 3 times, 3 x sc,*sc, inc* repeat 3 times (24)
R5: sl st in each st around (24)

Cut the thread and sew it.

Finishing cow

Embroider the nose holes to the nose and stuff it with fiberfill.
Pin the horns, the ears and the stuffed nose to the head and sew them.

Pig

Main color: orchid 0222, **color 1:** white 0106, **color 2:** raspberry 0256

Ears

Make 2. 2 x ch *with **main color***
R1: 4 x sc (4)
R2: *inc, sc* repeat 2 times (6)
R3: *inc, 2 x sc* repeat 2 times (8)
R4: *inc, 3 x sc* repeat 2 times (10)
R5: *inc, 4 x sc* repeat 2 times (12)
R6: *2 x sc, inc* repeat 4 times (16)
R7: *3 x sc, inc* repeat 4 times (20)

Close the opening with 9 x sl st,
cut the thread and sew it, see picture.

Nose

2 x ch *with **main color***
R1: 6 x sc (6)
R2: inc in each stitch around (12)
R3: *3 x sc, 3 x inc* repeat 2 times (18)
R4: Back loops only: sc in each stitch around (18)
R5: sc in each stitch around (18)
R6: sl st in each stitch around (18)

Cut the thread and sew it.

Finishing pig

Embroider the nose holes to the nose and stuff it with fiberfill.
Pin the stuffed nose and the ears to the head and sew them.

Ball

color 1: sky 0247, **color 2:** natural 0105, **color 3:** chocolate 0162
2 x ch with color 1
R1: 6 x sc (6)
R2: inc in each st around (12)
R3: *sc, inc* repeat 6 times (18)
R4: *2 x sc, inc* repeat 6 times (24)
R5: *3 x sc, inc* repeat 6 times (30)
R6: 2 x sc, inc, *4 x sc, inc* repeat 5 times, 2 x sc (36)
R7: *5 x sc, inc* repeat 6 times (42)
R8: 3 x sc, inc, *6 x sc, inc* repeat 5 times, 3 x sc (48)
R9: 47 x sc, sc with color change to **color 2** (48)
R10-18: sc in each st around (48)
R19: sc, sc with color change to **color 3**, 46 x sc (48)
R20: 3 x sc, dec, *6 x sc, dec* repeat 5 times, 3 x sc (42)
R21: *5 x sc, dec* repeat 6 times (36)
R22: 2 x sc, dec, *4 x sc, dec* repeat 5 times, 2 x sc (30)
R23: *3 x sc, dec* repeat 6 times (24)
R24: *2 x sc, dec* repeat 6 times (18) stuff the ball firmly
R25: *sc, dec* repeat 6 times (12)
R26: 6 x dec (6)

Cut the thread and sew it.

Eyes

Make 2. 2 x ch *with **color 1***
color 1: black 0110, **color 2:** flesh 0257, **color 3:** natural 0105
R1: 5 x sc, sc with color change to **color 2** (6)
R2: inc in each st around (12)

sl st, cut the thread

With **color 3** embroider a stitch to the eye, see picture.

Finishing ball

Sew the eyes to the ball and embroider the eyebrows and the mouth.

Fun and Easy Amigurumi

First published in 2015 by:

Neenom Publishing
an imprint of K and J Publishing
16 Whitegate Close
Swavesey, Cambridge, CB24 4TT
United Kingdom

ISBN: 978-1-910407-22-6

Editor: Robert F.A. Appelboom
Book Design: Will Dawes
Illustrations: Maria K. Windayani

Creators and copyright holders of the crochet patterns

Elizabeth Carr: Crochet Owl
Gemma Cubells: Vinnie, the Teddy Bear, Mr. Golden Sun and Merry, the Christmas Elf
Karin Godinez: Bowling Friends and Mia, the Monster Girl
Vanja Grundmann: Bear Bunnies and Lana Dolls
Viktorija Dineikiené: Helicopter
Teerapon Chan-lam (Jenny): Vicky the Bunny and Animal Friends
Rachel Hoe: Lil' Corgi Puppy, Lil' Spanish Wedding Dolls, Lil' Valentine's Teddy

Please contact Robert Appelboom on free.amigurumi.world@gmail.com for any questions about this wonderful book. Enjoy crocheting!

Printed in Great Britain
by Amazon